Paula Deen Celebrates!

Best Dishes and Best Wishes
for the Best Times
of Your Life

PAULA DEEN

WITH MARTHA NESBIT

SIMON & SCHUSTER

NEW YORK   LONDON   TORONTO   SYDNEY

SIMON & SCHUSTER
Rockefeller Center
1230 Avenue of the Americas
New York, NY 10020

Photographer's Assistant: Roy Galaday
Food Stylist: Michael Pederson
Assistant: Susan Vajaranant
Prop Stylist: Debrah E. Donahue
Assistant: Jayne Altaffer

SIMON & SCHUSTER and colophon are registered trademarks
of Simon & Schuster, Inc.

For information about special discounts for bulk purchases,
please contact Simon & Schuster Special Sales:
1-800-456-6798 or business@simonandschuster.com.

Manufactured in the United States of America

1   3   5   7   9   10   8   6   4   2

Library of Congress Cataloging-in-Publication Data
Deen, Paula H.
Paula Deen celebrates! : best dishes and best wishes for the best times of your life /
Paula Deen, with Martha Nesbit.
p.   cm.
1. Holiday cookery.   2. Menus.   I. Nesbit, Martha Giddens.   II. Title.
TX739.D44   2006
641.5'68—dc22   2006050457

ISBN-13: 978-0-7432-7811-9
ISBN-10:   0-7432-7811-9

Anthony, Michael, Paula, Jamie, Bobby, Michelle.

This is to my whole family—my old and my new family.
To my old family, thank you for your unwavering love and support.
To my new family, thank you for embracing me and my family,
allowing us to become one.

Acknowledgments

First, I would like to acknowledge my cookbook collaborator, Martha Nesbit, who has helped me translate my family favorites into recipes that can be enjoyed by others. Thanks to Brandon Branch, my personal assistant, for sharing his ideas for decorating for my celebrations, and to executive assistant Theresa Luckey and personal assistant Michelle White for handling all of the details of my professional life, as well as for assisting in the details of my personal life! Thanks to Russell Keutcher, merchandise manager for The Lady & Sons, who worked with Martha to get all of the old photos identified and sent to New York. Thanks to my agent, Barry Weiner, for believing in me, and my literary agent, Janis Donnaud, for her literary expertise. Once the cookbook is sent to New York, a whole bunch of folks take over up there—most important, our editor, Sydny Miner, who is just the smartest, nicest editor anyone could ever have. Helping Sydny was her assistant for most of the book, Sarah Hochman, who has just been promoted (congratulations, Sarah!). Also, Jackie Seow, the art director; the people who contributed to the photo shoot for the inserts: photographer Alan Richardson (he also shot the jacket), photographer's assistant Roy Galaday, food stylist Michael Pederson, assistant food stylist Susan Vajaranant, prop stylist Debrah E. Donahue, and Debrah's assistant, Jayne Altaffer. Also, designer Ellen Sasahara, production editor Sybil Pincus, copy editor Suzanne Fass, production manager Michelle Lomuscio, publicists Tracey Guest and Alexis Welby, publisher David Rosenthal, associate publishers Aileen Boyle and Deborah Darrock, president Carolyn Reidy, and CEO Jack Romanos.

Thank you, friends and family, including my restaurant family, for your patience. And to all the people who have crossed my life, I give special thanks for making me the person and the cook I am today.

Contents

Acknowledgments   vii

Introduction   1

New Year's Eve Brunch   5

New Year's Day Good Luck Meal   15

Elvis's Birthday   23

Valentine's Day   33

Presidents' Day   43

Big Easy Mardi Gras   49

My Wedding Anniversary   63

St. Patrick's Day   67

Easter Dinner   75

An Easter Egg Hunt   85

May Day Pink and White Party   95

Cinco de Mayo Fiesta   105

Mother's Day Tea   115

Graduation Potato Bar   123

Father's Day Boating Picnic   133

Fourth of July Outdoor Grill Party and Low-Country Boil   143

Movie-Watching Pizza Party in Bed   *153*

Thanksgiving   *163*

Sunday Afternoon Football Party   *179*

Homemade Christmas Gifts   *189*

Christmas Dinner   *203*

Metric Equivalencies   *213*

Index   *215*

Paula Deen
Celebrates!

Introduction

*H*ey, ya'll! In my last cookbook, Paula Deen & Friends, *I introduced ya'll* to a few of my girlfriends because I wanted them to share with ya'll how they put together menus for entertaining. In this book, I want to share with ya'll how *I* celebrate holidays and special occasions at my house along with my family. I need to tell ya up front that my first preference for entertaining is definitely casual, but that's not to say that when the old girl has to, she can't put on the dog.

When Michael and I were planning our dream house on Turner's Creek, on Wilmington Island near Savannah, we wanted our home to be inviting. I wanted all my guests to feel like they were being embraced when they came in. I really love large rooms, and fewer of them, rather than a lot of smaller rooms. Our downstairs consists of our master bedroom and bathroom and walk-in closet, a laundry room, a living room, a morning room, a foyer, and a huge kitchen that has two farmhouse tables in it. At one end is an antique table that seats twelve people; at the other end is a small table that seats four people. Michael and I sit at the smaller table when it's just the two of us, and when we have family and friends in, we go to the long table.

When Michael and I were building our kitchen, there were a few things that we just didn't want to do without. I had become so accustomed to commercial deep fryers in the restaurants that I felt like I just couldn't have a kitchen without one of those. I also felt like I couldn't cook without a convection oven like the ones we used in the restaurants. So, into my kitchen went two commercial pieces—the big convection oven and the deep fryer. I have a five-burner drop-in cooktop on my island, and then under the ventihood, I have another four burners, and two ovens and a double-size griddle for when I have the family over and I'm making pancakes or grilling sandwiches. So, I have really made my kitchen very user-friendly, and the way my kitchen is set up, a lot of us can get in there at the same time and we're not stepping on each other.

Outside, we have Michael's smokehouse—really an open-air kitchen. It's got all of his barbecue grills, and a long counter for holding lots of food and lots of dishes. We like to throw Low-Country boils there, and barbecue our chickens, grill briskets, cook steak, and smoke ribs. We always like company around us because we've found it's easier to cook for a crowd than to cook for just the two of us. Inside or out, I love to celebrate with family and friends and just stand around and chitchat and cook. And there's just nothing like cookin' and eatin' out by that water. It just gives you a huge appetite.

The important thing to me about this new book was the recipe selections. I didn't want ya'll to feel like you were seeing recipes that you had seen over and over and over again. Of course you'll find my favorites, but at the same time I wanted to give ya'll fresh, new recipes to add to your files. You know, there are so many different ways to update and freshen up recipes and I've said so many times, "A recipe is truly only a starting point." So, when it was time to start on this book, it was only natural that I would turn to my friend Martha Nesbit. Martha and I had worked on *Paula Deen & Friends: Living It Up, Southern Style,* and it was a very successful book. Martha and I see eye-to-eye on a great many things, and Martha's been testing recipes for twenty-five years. I know her and I trust her. She has taken my favorites, like my chicken potpie, and she's made sure the recipes will work in your kitchen for you just like they work in my kitchen for me 'cause you know that I do have a tendency to add a little of this and a little of that and by the time I get through with it, I don't know what's in it!

For ideas for decorating for my parties, I turned to my personal assistant, Brandon Branch. Brandon has a degree in horticulture from Mississippi State University, and he is the creative director for *Cooking with Paula Deen* magazine and the art director/prop stylist for *Paula's Home Cooking* and *Paula's Party,* both Food Network productions. Brandon also did the flowers for my wedding, for Jamie (Deen) and Brooke's wedding, and for Michelle (Groover) and Daniel Reed's wedding. Brandon and I are very, very close; we work very closely together, and he knows what I like. I just know you'll love his decorating tips.

Each celebration seemed to evoke a message, and I decided to share my thoughts with ya'll and call them "Paula's Pearls of Wisdom." I hope that maybe some of these Pearls will pop into your mind at the exact moment that you need them.

When I was planning this book, it was only natural that I turned to the men in my life to get their opinions as to what *they* consider my celebration food. I was so touched when I found out what they thought because I feel the exact same way—a celebration with your family doesn't have to mean a national holiday. In my house, a celebration can be something as simple as everybody being off from work at the same time. I have a daughter who is a nurse and one son who is home one week and works one week, and there's no juggling those kinds of schedules.

So, anyway, why don't we stop all the chitchat and get to cooking, 'cause we've got a lot to celebrate! Ya'll have fun, and, as always, I send you best dishes and love from my kitchen to yours.

Paula Deen

July 2006

New Year's Eve Brunch

*N*ew Year's Eve is probably my least favorite time to go out. What I really like is to spend the night at home—mine or someone else's. I want to be around old friends, not new people.

Billy and Kathy Lamas's house is the one stop we make—they live close by and we're usually home by midnight. Billy cooks the *best* standing rib roast on the grill and he serves the meat right off the grill just for me! Everyone brings a dish (usually the same one every year), and we have the most wonderful special foods that we all just look forward to digging into—shrimp dip, crab stew, steamed shrimp, and that dried beef and cream cheese dip that men just adore.

Rather than a heavy meal, I think hors d'oeuvres are nice for New Year's. Or, you can take it the other way as we have here, and have a late-night breakfast. Start the party after midnight, and your friends can make it their last stop on the way home. I always take our tree down before New Year's Eve, even though I keep up the rest of the decorations, like Christmas greenery and flowers. It's just an old superstition—my Granddaddy Paul wouldn't allow that tree to be in the house going into a New Year.

Paula's Pearls of Wisdom
Don't get caught up in having such a good time
that you make poor choices. Drink in moderation.

COLLARD GREEN WONTONS

We southerners love our greens! The melted cream cheese in the center of these crispy morsels is hot enough to burn your mouth if you pass them too quickly. Let these cool down on paper towels for about 5 minutes before serving, but don't let them sit too long for the tastiest results.

1 pound ham hocks, smoked turkey wings, or smoked neck bones
1 teaspoon House Seasoning, plus more for seasoning (page 147)
1 teaspoon seasoned salt
1 tablespoon hot sauce (my favorite is Texas Pete)
Olive oil, for drizzling

1. In a large pot, bring 1½ quarts water to a boil and add the meat, House Seasoning, seasoned salt, hot sauce, and a drizzle of olive oil. Cover, reduce the heat to medium, and cook for 1 hour.

2. Meanwhile, wash the collard greens thoroughly (or use prewashed greens, available in most supermarkets). Remove the thick stem that runs down the center of the greens by holding the stalk in one hand and stripping the leaves from the stalk with your other hand. Stack 6 to 8 leaves on top of each other, roll up,

½ large bunch collard greens
4 tablespoons (½ stick) butter
One 8-ounce package cream
  cheese, softened
70 wonton wrappers,
  approximately (1 package)
Peanut oil, for frying

and slice into ½- to 1-inch ribbons. Place the greens in the pot with the meat. Add the butter. Cook the greens, stirring occasionally, until the greens are tender, 45 minutes to 1 hour. When they are done, taste and adjust seasoning.

3. Remove the collard greens with a slotted spoon from the broth and transfer to a large bowl. Mix in the softened cream cheese.

4. To assemble, place a scant teaspoonful of the collard green mixture in the center of a wonton wrapper and fold into a triangle. Have a bowl of water ready— dip your finger in it and run it along the seams before pressing to seal. Repeat with the remaining wrappers. Place on a parchment- or wax-paper-lined baking sheet, covered with a damp paper towel, until ready to fry.

5. Heat 2 to 3 inches peanut oil in a heavy deep pot to 350°F. Fry the wontons in batches until they are golden brown, about 3 to 4 minutes per batch. Place on paper towels to drain and allow to cool for 5 minutes before serving.

Makes about 70 wontons

CRAB AND SPINACH CASSEROLE

This is a perfect dish if you love the combination of spinach and crabmeat, which I do.

Two 10-ounce packages
  frozen leaf spinach
½ cup (1 stick) butter
1 clove garlic, minced
2 tablespoons grated yellow
  onion
⅓ cup all-purpose flour
3 cups whole milk
  (*not* 1% or 2%)
1 cup (¼ pound) grated
  Swiss cheese
1 cup half-and-half
2 teaspoons fresh lemon juice
Pinch of garlic powder
Dash of freshly grated nutmeg
1 teaspoon salt
¼ teaspoon cayenne pepper
2 pounds fresh crabmeat,
  picked through twice
  for shells
1 cup fresh bread crumbs

1. Preheat the broiler. Butter a shallow 2-quart baking dish or eight ovenproof individual ramekins or scallop shells.

2. Thaw the spinach in its package in the refrigerator overnight or defrost in the microwave following the package directions. Remove the packaging and sauté the spinach in 2 tablespoons of the butter in a 12-inch skillet over medium heat with the garlic and onion for 3 minutes. Drain the spinach mixture and chop finely. Transfer the spinach to the baking dish.

3. Melt 4 tablespoons of the butter in a 2-quart saucepan. Stir in the flour and whisk until smooth. Over low heat, gradually add the milk, stirring constantly with a spoon until smooth and thickened, 8 to 10 minutes. When the sauce has thickened, add the cheese, half-and-half, lemon juice, garlic powder, nutmeg, salt, and cayenne. Cook over low heat until thickened again, about 10 minutes. Remove the sauce from the heat and carefully fold in the crabmeat.

4. Pour the mixture over the spinach. Sprinkle with the bread crumbs and dot with the remaining 2 tablespoons butter. (You may need more bread crumbs and butter if you are preparing individual ramekins.)

5. Broil about 5 minutes, until browned.

Serves 8

{ Note: This dish can be prepared ahead and refrigerated covered. When ready to cook, preheat the oven to 350°F and bake for about 30 minutes, until bubbly. Change the oven setting to broil and broil the top for about 5 minutes. }

BAKED TOMATOES

The topping is nice and spicy, the perfect contrast to the rich crabmeat. This recipe makes even winter tomatoes taste delicious.

4 ripe tomatoes
½ cup (1 stick) butter
2 cups fresh bread crumbs
¼ cup freshly grated Parmesan
   cheese
1 teaspoon Worcestershire
   sauce
1 teaspoon salt
½ teaspoon pepper
1 teaspoon dried thyme
¼ teaspoon hot sauce
   (I like Texas Pete)

1. Preheat the oven to 350°F.

2. Slice the stem ends off the tomatoes. Cut the tomatoes in half and place cut side up in a 13 by 9-inch baking dish.

3. In a 10-inch skillet over low heat, melt the butter. Stir in the bread crumbs, cheese, Worcestershire sauce, salt, pepper, thyme, and hot sauce. Place 2 tablespoons of the mixture over each tomato half.

4. Bake for 30 minutes, until the topping is browned.

Serves 8

HASH BROWN CASSEROLE

Well, you know how I love meat and potatoes, so I've used both sausage and prepared hash browns to make this eggy casserole an extra-hearty dish. I love that you have to make this ahead of time: at least eight hours or up to a day in advance.

I'd serve this for Sunday brunch anytime, with biscuits and a fresh fruit salad.

3 tablespoons butter

1 small yellow onion, chopped

4 cups frozen shredded hash browns

8 cups cubed French or Italian bread, crusts removed

1 pound bulk sausage, mild, hot, or sage

2 cups (½ pound) grated Gruyère cheese

2 cups (½ pound) freshly grated Romano cheese

2¼ cups whole milk

8 large eggs

1 teaspoon salt

¼ teaspoon pepper

¼ teaspoon freshly grated nutmeg

2 tablespoons Dijon mustard

1. Spray a deep 13 by 9-inch casserole with vegetable oil cooking spray. Melt the butter in a large frying pan. Add the onion and sauté over medium-low heat until soft, about 5 minutes. Add the hash browns and break apart. Sauté until soft, about 5 minutes. Place the bread cubes in the bottom of the casserole. Spread the onion and hash browns evenly over the bread cubes.

2. Sauté the sausage in the same pan as the potatoes, breaking apart large clumps. When the sausage is cooked through, remove it with a slotted spoon and distribute it evenly over the hash browns. Distribute the grated cheeses evenly over the sausage.

3. In a large mixing bowl, combine the milk, eggs, salt, pepper, nutmeg, and mustard, whisking briskly to blend. Pour over the cheese. Cover with plastic wrap and chill overnight or at least 8 hours.

4. Remove the casserole from the refrigerator 30 minutes before baking. Preheat the oven to 350°F. Bake the casserole, uncovered, for 45 to 50 minutes, until puffed and golden brown.

Serves 8 to 10

BLUEBERRY GEMS

These tender little muffins taste like dessert! The flavor of sweet fresh blueberries is just perfect with the rich crab casserole and spicy tomatoes. I don't have to tell ya just how important a colorful table is to me—and with the creamy white-and-green crab and spinach casserole, the bright red baked tomatoes, and these brown-and-blue blueberry muffins, I'm a happy girl.

2 cups self-rising flour
1½ cups sugar
2 eggs, lightly beaten
1 teaspoon vanilla extract
½ cup vegetable oil
½ cup whole milk
1 cup blueberries (preferably fresh, but frozen will work)

1. Preheat the oven to 375°F. Line 18 muffin tin cups with paper liners.

2. Combine the flour and sugar in a large bowl. In a smaller bowl, combine the eggs, vanilla, oil, and milk. Whisk together until well combined. Make a well in the center of the flour mixture. Pour in the liquid. Mix with a spoon until the flour is moistened. Gently fold in the blueberries.

3. Spoon the batter into the prepared muffin cups, filling about half to two-thirds full.

4. Bake for 23 to 25 minutes, until nicely browned and puffed.

Makes 18 muffins

PECAN PIE MUFFINS

What could be better than pecan pie? How about pecan pie muffins! These are great on any brunch table, and I like to bring them along on picnics, too.

½ cup (1 stick) butter, softened
¾ cup packed light brown sugar
2 eggs, beaten
½ cup all-purpose flour
¾ cup chopped pecans

1. Preheat the oven to 350°F. Grease and flour 8 muffin tin cups or use paper liners.

2. In a medium bowl, cream the butter and sugar. Add the eggs and mix well. Add the flour and stir until just combined. Stir in the pecans.

3. Spoon the batter into the prepared muffin cups, filling about two-thirds full.

4. Bake for 25 minutes. Serve warm with more butter!

Makes 8 muffins

HUMMINGBIRD CAKE

I like having a showstopping cake on the buffet table for special events. This old favorite is so easy—you just dump all of the ingredients into a bowl and stir!

3 cups self-rising flour

2 cups granulated sugar

¾ cup vegetable oil

½ cup finely chopped pecans

2 very ripe large bananas, mashed

One 8-ounce can crushed pineapple, with juice

1 teaspoon vanilla extract

1 teaspoon ground cinnamon

4 large eggs, beaten

ICING

One 1-pound box confectioners' sugar

One 8-ounce package cream cheese, at room temperature

6 tablespoons (¾ stick) butter, softened

1 teaspoon vanilla extract

1 tablespoon milk, or more, if needed

½ cup finely chopped pecans

1. Preheat the oven to 325°F.

2. Grease and flour three 8-inch round cake pans. In a large mixing bowl, combine the flour, sugar, oil, pecans, bananas, pineapple, vanilla, cinnamon, and eggs. Stir well with a spoon until the batter is smooth.

3. Pour the batter into the prepared pans. Bake for 26 to 28 minutes, until the tops spring back. Cool in the pans for about 10 minutes, then loosen from the pans and invert onto wire racks to cool completely.

4. To make the icing, mix the sugar, cream cheese, butter, vanilla, and 1 tablespoon milk in a large mixing bowl with an electric mixer until the icing is smooth. If needed, add more milk, 1 teaspoon at a time, to achieve the proper spreading consistency. Ice between the cake layers, and on the sides and top of the cake. Sprinkle the top with the pecans. Refrigerate until ready to serve.

Serves 12

MIMOSAS

This is such a lovely color, and the taste is refreshing—perfect with the seafood casserole.

FOR EACH DRINK

Orange juice

Champagne

Fresh mint sprig

Fill a champagne or wineglass half full with orange juice, then add champagne to fill. Garnish with a fresh mint sprig.

IRISH COFFEE

For coffee lovers, this is the best way to jump-start a new year.

FOR EACH DRINK

Lime slice

Sugar

¾ cup hot, strong black coffee

1 ounce Irish whiskey

2 tablespoons lightly whipped
   cream

Rub the lime slice around the rim of a glass coffee mug. Dip the rim in sugar to coat. Pour in the coffee. Add 1 to 2 teaspoons sugar and the whiskey and stir. Slide the whipped cream off a spoon so that it floats on top of the coffee.

❖ BRANDON'S DECORATING TIPS ❖

Paula always gets so much fruit over the holidays, and this New Year's Eve "brunch" is the perfect opportunity to put it to good use. Take green apples, hollow them out, and fill them with Sweetheart roses cut so only the blooms show. Hollow out lemons and limes, stick a votive candle in each one, and place them all around the house.

Paula also likes to have cut greens everywhere. In Savannah we can use greens from the garden; if you live where it's colder, evergreen garlands will do the trick. New year, new life—that's the idea.

New Year's Day Good Luck Meal

*I*f I don't cook any other day of the year, I cook on New Year's Day because the restaurants are closed (including mine!). And I am not going to let that day pass without my family consuming black-eyed peas, collard or turnip greens, and hog jowl. (My Granddaddy Paul's superstitions obviously made a big impression on me.) Black-eyed peas were for luck, and the greens represented financial success. The hog jowl was for health, believe it or not! In Savannah, every grocery store carries hog jowl, so we can always buy it; it's the favored meat for cooking greens and beans. A good, meaty hambone or streak o'lean will also do the trick. For New Year's, many southerners stick with a vegetable-only plate—black-eyed peas, greens, and corn bread. But the vegetables also taste delicious with a pork loin, like the recipe I've included.

Of course in my house there's always going to be a big old pot of rice to put those peas on. When black-eyed peas and rice are served together, we call it Hoppin' John. Some people even cook the two together, but then it gets mushy. If you don't like the traditional southern way of serving black-eyed peas, you can always have a black-eyed pea dip. I've included my recipe because I've served it quite a bit in my catering business and people seem to like it. It really doesn't matter how you get your black-eyed peas on New Year's Day; just make sure they are consumed in some form or fashion, please.

New Year's Day is a day when everybody may not be up to a huge celebration. Make it simple and enjoyable. The black-eyed peas and collard greens can be cooked two days ahead and reheated right before serving, and the topping for the ice cream can be done the day before or earlier in the day. Start the rice and corn bread right before you take the pork out of the oven.

With so many men in the family, New Year's Day at my house means lots of people sitting around watching the football games—they all have their favorite teams and there's a lot of hootin' and hollerin' going on. But this day is really about the food and I never alter my menu one bit. Here's a little tip: There's a real good chance you're not going to get any help from the guys on New Year's Day.

Paula's Pearls of Wisdom

Don't make your resolution to lose fifty pounds; make your resolution to lose ten pounds, or even twenty pounds. Be realistic about your resolutions. Don't set yourself up for failure.

HERB-CRUSTED PORK LOIN

The outside gets crusty and the inside is juicy and tender.

One 4-pound boneless pork
   loin, with fat left on
1 tablespoon salt
2 tablespoons olive oil
4 cloves garlic, minced
1 teaspoon dried thyme or
   2 teaspoons minced fresh
   thyme
1 teaspoon dried basil or
   2 teaspoons minced fresh
   basil
1 teaspoon dried rosemary or
   2 teaspoons minced fresh
   rosemary

1. Preheat the oven to 475°F.

2. Place the pork loin on a rack in a roasting pan. Combine the remaining ingredients in a small bowl. With your fingers, massage the mixture onto the pork loin, covering all of the meat and fat.

3. Roast the pork for 30 minutes, then reduce the heat to 425°F and roast for an additional hour. Test for doneness using an instant-read thermometer. When the internal temperature reaches 155°F, remove the roast from the oven. Allow it to sit for about 20 minutes before carving. It will continue to cook while it rests.

Serves 10 to 12

BLACK-EYED PEAS (FOR GOOD LUCK)
WITH HOG JOWL (FOR HEALTH)

Black-eyed peas are delicious served with the juices from the pot spooned over white rice, with minced green bell pepper as a garnish. Most southerners like to serve their peas with pepper sauce—vinegar mixed with hot peppers—a condiment found in the pickle aisle.

1 pound dried black-eyed
   peas
½ pound smoked meat—hog
   jowl, meaty ham hocks,
   smoked neckbones, or
   smoked ham
1 teaspoon salt
½ teaspoon pepper
4 tablespoons (½ stick) butter
½ cup finely chopped green
   bell pepper, for garnish
   (optional)
Pepper sauce, for seasoning at
   the table

1. In a large bowl, cover the peas with water and soak for 1 hour. Drain the peas and discard the soaking water.

2. Place the meat in a 2-quart saucepan and add 2½ cups water. Bring the water to a boil, then reduce the heat to medium-low. Cover the pot and cook the meat for 30 minutes. Add the salt and pepper and the peas to the meat and cook until the peas are soft and the liquid has thickened, about 45 minutes. When done, add the butter and serve. Garnish with green pepper, if desired. Serve with pepper sauce.

Serves 6 to 8

To make Hoppin' John: Sauté 1 chopped onion, 1 chopped green bell pepper, and 2 minced cloves garlic in 1 tablespoon vegetable oil until soft. Add 2 cups cooked black-eyed peas and 2 cups cooked white rice.

BLACK-EYED PEA DIP

This tastes like southern salsa—it's particularly refreshing in summer, but is a hit any time it's served.

Two 15-ounce cans black-eyed
  peas, drained
One 15-ounce can whole
  kernel corn, drained
One 10-ounce can Ro-Tel
  tomatoes or any spicy
  canned tomatoes, chopped
1 cup chopped red bell pepper
1 cup chopped green bell
  pepper
¼ cup chopped fresh jalapeño
  pepper
½ cup chopped yellow onion
One 4-ounce jar chopped
  pimientos, drained

DRESSING
½ cup red wine vinegar
1 tablespoon balsamic vinegar
1 teaspoon salt
½ teaspoon pepper
1 tablespoon Dijon mustard
¼ teaspoon sugar
Pinch of dried oregano
½ cup olive oil
½ cup vegetable oil
Corn chips, for serving

1. In a large bowl, combine the black-eyed peas, corn, tomatoes, red, green, and jalapeño peppers, onion, and pimientos.

2. In a glass jar with a tight-fitting lid, combine the wine and balsamic vinegars, salt, pepper, mustard, sugar, oregano, and olive and vegetable oils. Shake until the ingredients are blended.

3. Add the dressing to the pea mixture and stir gently but thoroughly. Cover and refrigerate until serving time. Allow to come to room temperature before serving. Stir well. Serve with corn chips.

Serves 10 to 12

COLLARD OR TURNIP GREENS
(FOR GOOD CASH FLOW)

Elvis was raised on greens, and so was I. I love my greens almost as much as I do Elvis! Collard and turnip greens are so gritty when they are first picked that washing them used to be the hardest part of cooking them. Now, groceries sell collards prewashed. Lots of people buy prewashed greens, but I still buy them by the bunch and wash 'em myself.

6 tablespoons (¾ stick) butter
1 large yellow onion, chopped
½ pound smoked meat—ham hocks, salt pork, smoked neckbones, or smoked ham
2 teaspoons House Seasoning (page 147)
1 teaspoon seasoned salt
One 1-pound bag prewashed collard or turnip greens or 1 large bunch collard or turnip greens, well washed, ribs removed, and leaves sliced into 1-inch ribbons
1 tablespoon bacon grease (optional)

1. In a 3-quart saucepan, melt 2 tablespoons of the butter over medium-high heat. Add the onion and sauté until it begins to soften, about 3 minutes. Add 2½ cups water and the smoked meat, House Seasoning, and seasoned salt. Bring to a boil, cover, then reduce the heat and allow the meat to cook for 30 minutes.

2. Add the greens—they will fill the pot, but they will cook down very quickly. Bring to a boil, then reduce the heat to low, cover the pot, and cook the greens until they are tender, 20 to 40 minutes, depending on how young and tender they are and how tender you like your greens.

3. Add the bacon grease, if using, and the remaining 4 tablespoons butter. Taste and adjust seasoning.

Serves 8 to 10

{ Note: When you reheat the leftovers, add 2 tablespoons Texas Pete hot sauce. Yip-pee! }

CORN BREAD MUFFINS

These are your basic old muffins. Southerners have to have them so we can sop up all of those terrific juices from the peas and greens. For real down-home flavor, use bacon grease, but you can substitute vegetable oil.

Vegetable shortening
2 cups plain yellow cornmeal
   (not self-rising)
1 tablespoon sugar
1 tablespoon baking powder
1 teaspoon salt
1 egg, beaten
1¼ cups whole milk
3 tablespoons bacon grease,
   warmed until liquefied, or
   3 tablespoons vegetable oil
Butter, at room temperature,
   for serving

1. Preheat the oven to 475°F. Generously grease 12 muffin tin cups with vegetable shortening.

2. In a medium bowl, combine the cornmeal, sugar, baking powder, and salt. Stir well. Add the egg, milk, and bacon grease or vegetable oil. Stir the batter well with a spoon.

3. Pour the batter into the prepared muffin cups, filling about half full. Bake for 18 minutes, until the corn muffins are puffed and browned. Serve with soft butter.

Makes 12 muffins

RUM RAISIN–APPLE TOPPING FOR ICE CREAM

Apples and pork just seem to go together. We can eat ice cream at my house anytime, summer or winter. This warm topping goes over the cold ice cream and makes it melt into a yummy puddle. If Michael and I are eating plain ice cream, we'll usually choose pralines and cream or turtle or butter pecan. But for this topping, nothing but French vanilla will do.

2 tablespoons (¼ stick) butter
5 Granny Smith apples,
   peeled, cored, and thinly
   sliced
1 cup sugar
1 teaspoon ground cinnamon
½ cup golden raisins
1 tablespoon rum
2 tablespoons cornstarch

Melt the butter in a 2-quart saucepan. Add the apples. Stir in the sugar, cinnamon, and raisins. Cook over low heat until the apples are tender, about 5 minutes. Combine the rum and cornstarch and add to the apples. Cook for 1 minute to thicken. Serve warm over ice cream.

Serves 8

❖ BRANDON'S DECORATING TIPS ❖

In Savannah, we are lucky enough to have camellias blooming at New Year's, so I take lots of square vases and fill them with boxwood clippings and white camellias. And, please, *never* leave foliage below the waterline. That's one of my pet peeves. It promotes bacteria growth in the water and makes it cloudy, and shortens the life of the flowers.

Elvis's Birthday

*E*lvis's *Birthday, for those of you who don't know this "holiday," is January* 8, 1935.

I just adored Elvis. When I was thirteen, I used to hold his album covers up and have my picture taken with them, like we were standing there together! I went to see *Love Me Tender* thirteen times; I could almost say the dialogue along with the movie. I felt very close to Elvis because he had vacationed at one of my Grandmother and Grandaddy Paul's places—Magnolia Hunting and Fishing Lodge in Crystal River, Florida—and Elvis had written them a postcard himself, thanking them for a wonderful time. In the sixth grade, I took the postcard to school because I wanted everybody to see it, and somebody stole it from my purse. I was devastated!

Elvis really liked very simple, basic food—grits, cabbage, fried chicken, corn bread, country-fried steak, meat loaf, mashed potatoes, and biscuits, and plenty of country gravy. He liked hamburgers well-done. He loved peanut butter and banana sandwiches fried in butter, and freshly sliced tomatoes with just about any meal. At Graceland, he insisted on having fresh banana pudding and brownies available at all times! He was a real fan of comfort food.

If I were throwing a birthday party for the King, I'd invite my guitar-playing friends to bring their guitars, and I'd tell everyone to come dressed fifties style—the men with their hair slicked back and the women with poodle skirts, bobby socks, and oxfords. We'd play all of Elvis's albums, and eat this delicious comfort meal.

Paula's Pearls of Wisdom

Elvis's roots ran very deep when it came to the love of his family and his home. Everything those two things meant were probably missed by him when fame took over his life and took him away from home. No matter where he roamed, he knew that there was no place like home . . . or home cookin'!

COUNTRY-FRIED STEAK WITH GRAVY

Chicken-fried steak is cubed steak floured, fried, and served with white gravy. Country-fried steak is cubed steak floured, fried, and served with a brown gravy, often with onions. Both are delicious, stick-to-your-ribs dishes.

8 to 10 pieces cubed steak
(about 2½ pounds)
Salt and pepper
1 cup all-purpose flour
¼ cup vegetable oil
1 large yellow onion, sliced
into thin rings
3 beef bouillon cubes or
two 10.75-ounce cans
condensed beef broth or
3 teaspoons granulated
beef bouillon

1. Generously season the meat on both sides with salt and pepper. Place the flour in a resealable plastic bag and add the steak to the bag, several pieces at a time, shaking to coat all sides. Place the floured meat on a piece of waxed paper next to the cooktop.

2. Pour the oil into a heavy flat-bottomed 12-inch skillet with a tight-fitting lid. Heat the oil over medium-high heat for about a minute, then add the steak pieces. Brown the meat on each side until crispy and dark brown, about 3 minutes per side. It may all fit into the skillet, or you may have to brown the meat

in two batches. After browning, place all the meat in the skillet and reduce the heat to low. Distribute the onion rings over the top of the meat.

3. Dissolve the bouillon cubes or granulated bouillon in 2½ cups water, or use the canned broth. Pour the beef bouillon over the meat and onions. Place the lid on the skillet, and cook over very low heat for about 45 minutes, until the meat is tender and the gravy has thickened.

4. Serve over white rice.

Serves 6 to 8

WHITE RICE

This is such a simple dish, but we southerners could eat white rice twice a day. Of course, I make mine with half a stick of butter!

1½ teaspoons salt
4 tablespoons (½ stick) butter
1½ cups white rice

In a 2-quart pot with a tight-fitting lid, place 3 cups water and the salt and butter. Bring the water to a rolling boil. Add the rice, stirring well. Place the lid on the pot and reduce the heat to the lowest setting possible. The rice will be ready to eat in 18 minutes.

Serves 6 to 8

COUNTRY CABBAGE

Some people like their cabbage crunchy, but in the South we like it cooked until it's tender.

3 slices bacon
¾ of a medium (about
  2 pounds) head of
  cabbage, cored and cut
  into chunks about the size
  of a golf ball
1½ teaspoons salt
½ teaspoon pepper
2 tablespoons (¼ stick) butter
  (or more!)

1. In a large heavy-bottomed stockpot with a lid, fry the bacon until it is crisp. Remove the bacon to paper towels, drain, crumble, and set aside.

2. Add 1 cup water to the bacon grease. Add the cabbage. Bring to a boil and add the salt and pepper. Place the lid on the pot and reduce the heat to medium. Allow the cabbage to cook for 10 to 15 minutes, until it is to your liking.

3. Remove the pot from the heat. Add the butter and stir until it is melted. Add the reserved crumbled bacon and stir.

Serves 6 to 8

BUTTERMILK BISCUITS

Use these biscuits to sop up the gravy from the country-fried steak, the juices from the cabbage, or both!

2 cups self-rising flour
2 teaspoons sugar
½ cup vegetable shortening
⅔ cup buttermilk

1. Preheat the oven to 450°F.

2. In a bowl, combine the flour and sugar. Using two knives, cut in the shortening until it is thoroughly combined. You may also use a food processor. Add the buttermilk all at once and stir until it and the flour are mixed. The dough will be very moist.

3. Using a floured board and floured fingertips, pat out the dough to a ½-inch thickness. Cut the dough into 12 biscuits with a sharp knife, dipping the knife in flour after each use to keep it from sticking.

4. Transfer the biscuits with a floured metal spatula to an ungreased baking sheet and bake for 10 to 12 minutes, until the tops are lightly browned. Serve warm.

Makes 12

OLD-FASHIONED BANANA PUDDING

There are dozens of recipes for banana pudding, but this is the one that's the classic.

One 12-ounce box vanilla
    wafers
⅓ cup unsifted cornstarch
⅔ cup sugar
¼ teaspoon salt
3 cups whole milk
3 eggs
1 teaspoon vanilla extract
2 tablespoons (¼ stick) butter,
    cut up
5 perfectly ripe bananas
1 cup whipping cream,
    whipped with ¼ cup
    confectioners' sugar

1. Line the bottom and sides of a 13 by 9-inch glass casserole with about half of the vanilla wafers.

2. Mix the cornstarch, sugar, and salt in the top of a double boiler. Slowly add the milk and cook over simmering water until the mixture is thick, 12 to 15 minutes, stirring constantly.

3. Beat the eggs in a small heatproof glass dish and add about ¼ cup of the hot milk mixture to the eggs. Stir, then add the eggs to the double boiler. Cook for 1 minute more. (The custard should be about the consistency of mayonnaise. If it is not, keep stirring over simmering water until it thickens.) Add the vanilla and butter and stir until combined. Turn off the heat, transfer the custard to a bowl, place a piece of plastic wrap directly on the pudding to prevent a skin from forming, and allow the pudding to cool to room temperature.

4. Slice a generous layer of bananas over the vanilla wafers. Cover with about half the pudding. Repeat the layers—vanilla wafers, bananas, and pudding. Top with a thick layer of whipped cream. Serve at room temperature, or cover with plastic wrap and chill.

Serves 10 to 12

ELVIS PEANUT BUTTER GOOEY BUTTER CAKES

Gooey butter cakes are one of my specialties, and they're one of the most popular items on The Lady & Sons menu. I can't tell you how many varieties of gooey butter cakes we've served over the years! This one was sent to us by Brian Proffitt of Lexington, Kentucky. It would be pretty good with a chocolate crust, too.

CAKE LAYER

One 18.25-ounce package
   yellow cake mix

1 egg

½ cup (1 stick) butter, melted

FILLING

One 8-ounce package cream
   cheese, softened

3 eggs

1 teaspoon vanilla extract

½ cup creamy peanut butter

1 ripe banana, mashed with
   a fork or potato masher

½ cup (1 stick) butter

One 1-pound box
   confectioners' sugar

GARNISH

1 cup whipping cream,
   whipped with 1 tablespoon
   confectioners' sugar

Mint leaves

1. Preheat the oven to 350°F. Spray a 13 by 9-inch baking pan with vegetable oil cooking spray.

2. In a large mixing bowl, stir together the cake mix, egg, and butter with a fork, mixing well. Pat lightly into the prepared pan.

3. To prepare the filling, in the same large mixing bowl, beat the cream cheese, eggs, and vanilla. Add the peanut butter, banana, and butter and beat well. Stir in the confectioners' sugar with a spatula, then beat until the mixture is smooth, about 2 minutes. Pour the batter over the cake mixture.

4. Bake for 45 to 50 minutes. You want the center to still be a little loose, so do not overbake. Allow to cool about 15 minutes before slicing.

5. Top each warm cake slice with a dollop of whipped cream and a mint leaf.

Makes 16 squares

FRIED PEANUT BUTTER AND BANANA SANDWICH

I wouldn't serve this as a part of my Elvis meal, but I wanted to share this recipe because it was one of Elvis's favorites! If you've got kids in the house, this would be a real treat on a Saturday morning.

2 slices white bread
2 tablespoons creamy peanut
  butter
1 small ripe banana
2 tablespoons (¼ stick) butter

Spread 1 slice of the bread with the peanut butter. Slice the banana evenly over the peanut butter. Top with the second slice of bread. Spread the outside of the bread with the butter. Fry the sandwich in a small skillet over medium heat until the bread is browned on both sides.

Serves 1

❖ **BRANDON'S DECORATING TIPS** ❖

The King had a style all his own, but I'd go elegant rather than over the top.
Take a big crystal bowl, line it with any green foliage that's available
from your yard, and fill it with beautiful bright yellow and green bananas.
Elvis loved bananas.

Valentine's Day

*V*alentine's Day is a night for lovers and the one day at the restaurant that I take reservations for tables for two.

This celebration is just for me and Michael. Michael's job is to make sure that I have a big bouquet of flowers, and my job is to make him a delicious meal. Some of his favorite foods are shrimp, lobster, steak, and chocolate, so I'll make my version of surf-'n'-turf and something rich and decadent for dessert. 'Course, his very favorite food is oxtails, but that's not a very romantical (that's Michael's word) meal and it's messy to eat. This Valentine's Day, I'll probably set us a table in our private garden and have a fireplace going—real romantic and intimate. After dinner we'll head to the hot tub with some motion lotion!

Some of these recipes appeared in the January/February 2006 issue of *Cooking with Paula Deen* and they are just wonderful! Save any of the leftovers for a delicious lunch. I'm giving you choices for both the appetizer and the dessert.

If I was short on time, I would not be above buying a really high-quality dessert. But both of these rich chocolate treats—especially if you serve them warm with vanilla ice cream—will end your meal with a bang!

Paula's Pearls of Wisdom
*Don't forget to get dolled up! He'll think
you're hotter than a June bride in a feather bed!*

THE LADY & SONS CRAB-STUFFED SHRIMP

I've been asked over and over to publish this recipe in one of my books. Well, ya'll, here it is!

1 tablespoon butter

3 green onions, finely chopped

½ cup finely chopped green
    bell pepper

¼ teaspoon garlic powder

¼ cup whipping cream

1 tablespoon Dijon mustard

Dash of cayenne pepper

½ cup saltine cracker crumbs

¼ cup mayonnaise

1 egg

2 tablespoons minced fresh
    parsley

1. Preheat the oven to 350°F.

2. Melt the butter in a large skillet over medium heat and sauté the green onions, green pepper, and garlic powder until the pepper is limp. Place in a mixing bowl and add the cream, mustard, and cayenne pepper. Mix well.

3. Add the cracker crumbs, mayonnaise, egg, parsley, and lemon juice. Mix well. Gently fold in the crabmeat.

4. Split the shrimp down the bottom center to the tail, being careful not to cut through the back. Stuff each shrimp with a small mound of the crabmeat mixture. Wrap the shrimp in bacon and secure with

Juice of ½ lemon

1 pound crabmeat, picked
through twice for shells

1 pound extra-large or jumbo
shrimp, peeled (tails on)
and deveined

12 slices bacon, halved
crosswise

BASIL CREAM SAUCE

2 tablespoons (¼ stick) butter

1 tablespoon olive oil

1 teaspoon minced garlic

3 tablespoons minced yellow
onion

¼ cup white wine

2 cups whipping cream

1 chicken bouillon cube,
crushed, or 1 teaspoon
granulated bouillon

3 tablespoons store-bought
basil pesto

a toothpick. Place the shrimp on a baking sheet and cook in the top third of the oven for 15 to 20 minutes, until the bacon is cooked through. Turn the oven to broil and broil for 4 minutes to crisp the bacon.

5. While the shrimp are cooking, make the Basil Cream Sauce: Heat the butter and olive oil in a skillet over medium heat. Add the garlic and onion and cook until light brown, about 3 minutes. Add the wine and reduce by half. Add the cream and bouillon cube or granulated bouillon and reduce by half again. Add the pesto, bring to a simmer, and heat until slightly thickened, about 2 to 3 minutes.

6. To serve, arrange 4 shrimp on each plate. Drizzle the shrimp with the Basil Cream Sauce.

Serves 5

SHRIMP AND LOBSTER BISQUE

We just can't get enough seafood at my house, and living in Savannah, we get the freshest catch. This creamy soup has such a beautiful soft pink color, and the flavor is so rich and delicious.

2 steamed fresh lobster tails,
    about 8 ounces total
4 tablespoons (½ stick) butter
1 small white onion, finely
    chopped
2 celery stalks, finely chopped
2 cloves garlic, minced
⅓ cup all-purpose flour
2 cups chicken broth
½ pound steamed medium
    shrimp, peeled and
    deveined
2 cups half-and-half
1 teaspoon Creole seasoning

1. Remove the lobster meat from the shells, chop it coarsely, and set aside.

2. In a large saucepan, melt the butter over medium heat and sauté the onion, celery, and garlic until soft, about 5 minutes. Stir in the flour with a whisk until it is smooth. Slowly add the chicken broth and allow it to cook until thickened, about 10 minutes.

3. Add the shrimp and lobster meat. Turn off the heat and allow the mixture to cool. When it is no longer steaming, process the soup in a food processor or blender until smooth.

4. Return the soup to the saucepan over medium heat and add the half-and-half and Creole seasoning. Heat through, but do not boil.

Serves 6

STUFFED BEEF TENDERLOIN

When I really want to please Michael, I prepare a good piece of beef.

One 1½-pound beef
   tenderloin
1 tablespoon butter
¼ cup chopped shallots
   or yellow onion
1 cup chopped fresh
   mushrooms
Salt and pepper
Soy sauce

1. Preheat the oven to 400°F.

2. Butterfly the beef tenderloin by cutting the beef lengthwise down the center to within ½ inch of the other side. Set the beef aside.

3. In a medium skillet, melt the butter and cook the shallots or onion over low heat until tender, about 5 minutes. Add the mushrooms and cook over low heat about 5 minutes, or until the liquid is reduced by half.

4. To stuff the tenderloin, open the beef and sprinkle the inside with salt and pepper and rub with the soy sauce. Spoon the mushroom mixture down the center of the tenderloin. Bring the two sides of the tenderloin up around the filling to meet. Using butcher string, tie the tenderloin together at 2-inch intervals. Place the tenderloin in a roasting pan. Roast for 45 minutes for medium rare (150°F on a meat thermometer). Let stand for 10 minutes before slicing. Slice about 1½ inches thick.

Serves 2, with leftovers

GARLIC MASHED POTATOES

Garlic mashed potatoes are all the rage in restaurants everywhere. And why not? They are terrific with beef dishes!

3 medium baking potatoes, peeled and coarsely chopped
1 teaspoon salt
4 tablespoons (½ stick) butter, at room temperature
¼ cup sour cream, at room temperature
1 teaspoon finely minced garlic
Whole milk, start with 1 tablespoon, at room temperature or warmed
Salt and pepper

1. In a medium saucepan, cook the potatoes in salted water until tender, about 15 minutes. Drain the potatoes and return them to the saucepan.

2. Add the butter, sour cream, and garlic. Mash the potatoes with a potato masher or the back of a fork until the ingredients are blended. Add the milk, 1 tablespoon at a time, until the potatoes are the desired consistency. Taste, and add salt and pepper if needed.

Serves 2, with leftovers

PHYLLO-WRAPPED ASPARAGUS

These are beautiful to look at and very tasty, too!

8 or 9 asparagus spears
4 sheets frozen phyllo (filo)
　　pastry from a 16-ounce
　　package, thawed and
　　covered with a clean, damp
　　tea towel
4 tablespoons (½ stick) butter,
　　melted
¼ cup freshly grated Parmesan
　　cheese

1. Preheat the oven to 375°F. Snap off the tough ends of the asparagus.

2. Unwrap the phyllo pastry and cut the stack in half lengthwise. Remove 4 sheets of pastry. Reserve the rest for another use; store in an airtight freezer bag. Cover the phyllo lightly with a damp tea towel to keep it from drying out.

3. Take 1 piece of phyllo and brush lightly with melted butter. Sprinkle with cheese. Place 2 or 3 asparagus spears on the short end of the phyllo. Roll up, jelly-roll style. Fold over the ends to enclose the asparagus spears.

4. Place each roll, seam side down, on a baking sheet. Brush with butter and sprinkle with cheese. Repeat until all of the asparagus spears are rolled. Bake for 15 to 18 minutes or until golden brown and crispy.

Serves 2

MOLTEN LAVA CAKES

Michael Marcus is my friend and the makeup artist for my magazine—not that I need one (tee hee!). It turns out that Michael loves to cook, and this is one of his favorite recipes that he wanted to share with me. I love to top everything with whipped cream or ice cream. Why not?

Six 1-ounce squares
    bittersweet chocolate
Two 1-ounce squares
    semisweet chocolate
10 tablespoons (1¼ sticks)
    butter
½ cup all-purpose flour
1½ cups confectioners' sugar
3 large eggs
3 egg yolks
1 teaspoon vanilla extract
2 tablespoons Grand Marnier
Whipped cream or ice cream

1. Preheat the oven to 425°F. Grease six 6-ounce custard cups.

2. Melt the chocolates and butter in the microwave at full power for 1 minute or in a double boiler over simmering water until melted. If microwaving, check the chocolate after 1 minute, stir, and continue microwaving for 10 seconds, until melted. Transfer the chocolate mixture to a large mixing bowl.

3. Add the flour and sugar to the chocolate mixture. Stir in the eggs and egg yolks until the mixture is smooth. Stir in the vanilla and Grand Marnier. Divide the batter evenly among the custard cups. Place the cups on a baking sheet.

4. Bake for 13 minutes. The edges will be firm, but the center should be runny. Run a knife around the edges to loosen and invert onto dessert plates. Serve with whipped cream or ice cream.

Makes 6 cakes

{ Note: You'll need only two of these rich cakes for Valentine's. Refrigerate the leftovers in a plastic bag and use within a week. They may also be frozen. Allow to thaw, then reheat gently in the microwave (30 seconds at 50% power). Serve with ice cream. }

CHOCOLATE BUNDLES WITH CHOCOLATE SAUCE

Frozen puff pastry is really a cook's good friend; you can create so many wonderful dishes with so little effort! When I make these for Michael, I use miniature Snickers—his favorite candy bar—for the filling. Choose your sweetie's favorite candy; he (or she!) will appreciate the thought.

BUNDLES

1 sheet frozen puff pastry
   dough
2 eggs
1 teaspoon whipping cream
8 chocolate Kisses
8 miniature chocolate
   candy bars

CHOCOLATE SAUCE

½ cup whipping cream
4 ounces milk chocolate,
   broken into small pieces
Sweetened whipped cream
   (optional)
Sliced fresh strawberries,
   for garnish
Mint sprigs, for garnish

1. Preheat the oven to 350°F. Line a cookie sheet with parchment paper.

2. To make the bundles, allow the puff pastry to thaw, covered, for 30 minutes at room temperature. When it is pliable, unfold the pastry and cut the sheet into four 4 by 4-inch squares.

3. Beat the eggs and cream together to make an egg wash. Brush the entire surface of each pastry square with the egg wash. In the center of each pastry square, place 2 chocolate Kisses and 2 mini candy bars. Pull the corners of each square up around the chocolate, and twist the top of the dough clockwise to complete the "bundle." Brush the exteriors of the chocolate bundles with more egg wash.

4. Place the bundles on the cookie sheet. Bake about 35 minutes, until golden brown.

5. To make the chocolate sauce: In a small saucepan, bring the cream to a boil. Place the chocolate pieces in a bowl and pour the hot cream over the top. Whisk until the sauce is smooth.

6. Puddle the chocolate sauce on a plate and place a bundle on top. Top with whipped cream and additional chocolate sauce, if desired. Serve the bundles garnished with strawberry slices and mint sprigs.

Makes 4 chocolate bundles

❖ BRANDON'S DECORATING TIPS ❖

Nothing says Valentine's Day like roses. Paula and I are both in love with red roses. To keep roses fresh, here's a little secret: Cut them at an angle under water—that way, the rose soaks up water instead of air. That will prevent that droopy-head thing.

Set your table with good linen and china, then sprinkle the table with rose petals. Wrap your napkins with ivy and tuck in a sprig of jasmine. Put tea lights or votive candles everywhere.

If you've got a fireplace, get it going, and have the hot tub bubbling.

Presidents' Day

*J*immy Carter is definitely my favorite president, and it's not because he's from the South, ya'll, but because of the kind of man he is and what he represents. He does so much good for people. He's smart. He's the epitome of a true southern gentleman. In my opinion, he's the greatest humanitarian walking the earth today. He gives so much back to the people he loves.

You just have to admire who he is and what he stands for. Two things that I've done are really up there. One was the day I got to share my story with Oprah and do her show, and the other was being with Mr. Jimmy in Plains, Georgia, something I have

With my favorite president. Hail to the chef!

actually done twice! The latest time was in January of 2006, when my crew went to Plains to film one of my Food Network shows right in Mr. Jimmy's own kitchen! I felt like I was fifteen years old again—I was almost kind of shy. The first time, when we were getting ready to film, I put my arm through his and said, "What should I call you?" He said, "Call me Jimmy," and I said, "Oh, no! My daddy wouldn't like that. I'll call you Mr. Jimmy." He said, "That's fine."

Mr. Jimmy is like me. He likes traditional southern food. He loves his fried chicken and southern staples. One of his favorite things is the Strawberry Cheese Ring that's in my first cookbook.

While we were in Plains, the people were so gracious to us. We had a wonderful supper prepared by Jack and Charlotte Vineyard, with all of the desserts prepared by their daughter, Melanie. The ladies of the Plains Better Hometown Program treated us to breakfast, and Maggie Crimes, one of Mr. Jimmy's favorite cooks, showed us how to dish up her delicious southern food at Mom's Kitchen. Then, as if we weren't already stuffed, Bobby Salter of Plain Peanuts fed us again, topping off the day with his famous peanut butter ice cream. Yum!

Presidents' Day is a great time to honor the men who have stepped into the position of being America's leader. They totally give up their lives to do that, and anybody willing to take on that job is pretty amazing, don't ya think?

Paula's Pearls of Wisdom

This message is for mothers of sons: Pray that we can instill truth, honor, and gentleness as well as Miss Lillian did in her son, Jimmy Carter.

This menu is inspired by my visits to Plains. Cream is in everything, isn't it? The thing is, these just happened to be the best recipes from the trips to Plains.

MENU

Oyster-Stuffed Quail
Penny Smith's Sausage Casserole
Whipping-Cream Grits
Creamy Cabbage
Peanut Butter Ice Cream
Easy Peach Ice Cream

OYSTER-STUFFED QUAIL

Southern hunters typically like to fry their quail and serve them crisp, or make a gravy and serve them smothered. This recipe combines crispy quail and one of my favorite foods—oysters.

4 quail, semi-boneless
Garlic salt
Seasoned salt
¼ cup vegetable oil
12 small oysters
Melted butter

1. Preheat the oven to 400°F.

2. Wash the quail and pat them dry. Season them inside and out with garlic salt and seasoned salt. Heat the oil in a skillet with an ovenproof handle over medium-high heat and sear the quail on all sides. Dip the oysters in melted butter and distribute them inside the cavity of the birds.

3. Place the skillet with the stuffed quail in the oven and roast for 25 minutes, until brown and crispy.

Serves 4

PENNY SMITH'S SAUSAGE CASSEROLE

This spicy casserole is delicious with the quail for dinner, or the next morning for a pre-hunt breakfast. Penny Smith, manager of the Georgia Visitor Information Center in Plains, was one of our hostesses.

1 pound bulk sausage, sage or spicy, your preference

1 small yellow onion, chopped

1 green or red bell pepper, chopped

8 ounces mushrooms, sliced

12 eggs

½ cup (2 ounces) grated Cheddar cheese

2 tomatoes, diced

½ teaspoon dried thyme or 1 teaspoon minced fresh thyme

Salsa, for garnish

Jalapeño peppers, fresh or pickled, finely chopped, for garnish

1. Preheat the oven to 350°F.

2. Break up the sausage and sauté it in a large frying pan until it is no longer pink. Add the onion, bell pepper, and mushrooms and sauté until the vegetables are limp, 3 to 5 minutes. Beat the eggs, then add them to the frying pan with the sausage and vegetables and soft-scramble the eggs.

3. Transfer the mixture to a 13 by 9-inch baking dish. Sprinkle the cheese over the eggs. Distribute the diced tomatoes evenly over the cheese. Sprinkle with the thyme.

4. Bake for 20 minutes. Serve warm with salsa and jalapeño peppers.

Serves 6 to 8

WHIPPING-CREAM GRITS

It's hard to make grits better than they already are, but whipping cream and butter does it!

½ cup regular grits (not instant
    or quick grits)
1 teaspoon salt
4 tablespoons (½ stick) butter,
    at room temperature
¼ cup whipping cream, at
    room temperature

1. In a nonstick saucepan with a lid, bring 2 cups water to a boil. Stir in the grits and salt and whisk well. Place the lid on the pot, reduce the heat to the lowest possible temperature, and cook for 10 to 12 minutes, until the grits are thick.

2. When the grits are thick, stir in the butter and whipping cream. Serve immediately.

Serves 4

CREAMY CABBAGE

A little bacon and whipping cream turn cabbage into a gourmet dish.

4 slices bacon, cut in slivers
One 10-ounce package
    shredded cabbage
1 chicken bouillon cube,
    crushed, or 1 teaspoon
    granulated bouillon
¼ cup whipping cream

Sauté the bacon in a medium saucepan until it is crisp and the fat has been rendered. Add the cabbage to the pot, along with the bouillon cube and ½ cup water. Cover and cook over low heat for 3 to 4 minutes, until tender. Stir in the whipping cream and serve hot.

Serves 4

PEANUT BUTTER ICE CREAM

Bobby Salter, who owns the Plain Peanuts gift shop, makes delicious peanut butter ice cream. We formulated a recipe that can be made in one of the smaller (1½-quart) ice cream freezers.

½ cup creamy peanut butter
1 cup whole milk
1 cup whipping cream
2 cups half-and-half
¾ cup sugar
1 teaspoon vanilla extract

In a small bowl, whisk together the peanut butter and milk until blended. Stir in the rest of the ingredients and freeze in an ice cream maker according to the manufacturer's instructions. Serve immediately, or store in the freezer in a plastic container with a snap-on lid.

Makes about eight ½-cup servings

EASY PEACH ICE CREAM

Jimmy Carter loves peach ice cream, and Penny Smith discovered an easy way to make store-bought ice cream taste like fresh-churned!

1 gallon vanilla ice cream
1 quart fresh peaches, peeled, stoned, and halved
1 cup sugar
1 teaspoon almond extract

Allow the ice cream to soften. Puree the peaches in a blender with the sugar and almond extract. Stir into the ice cream. Refreeze in a plastic container with a snap-on lid.

Makes 1½ gallons

Big Easy Mardi Gras

A Tribute to the Food of New Orleans

*W*ho will ever forget the devastation caused by Hurricane Katrina, which hit New Orleans with 145-mile-an-hour winds on August 29, 2005, displacing more than one million families? For seven long days Michael and I paced the floor, watching the news, just hoping to get a glimpse of Michael's brother, Father Hank Groover, a Dominican friar and Catholic priest stationed at St. Anthony of Padua on Canal Street. We didn't know if he was dead or alive. Finally, on the seventh day, he called us. He told us that because his house was on one of the highest lots on Canal Street, more than sixty people had taken refuge there—some with their pets. When

Michael's brother Father Hank Groover.

the first floor flooded, they moved to the second and third floors. Hank would wade in the streets, looking for survivors. He found a ninety-two-year-old woman floating on her mattress in her bedroom! "I can't find my walker," she told Hank. A group of volunteers pushed a boat right into her bedroom in chest-deep water, loaded her up, and brought her to join the others in the Canal Street house. After the fourth day, with the water still rising, they all evacuated to the Interstate, where Hank waited for three days for transportation to Houston. He said as tragic as the circumstances were, he met wonderful people, and he tells stories full of humor and heroism and was amazed at the way people pitched in to help others.

Months after the devastation, I asked a precious little boy, the nephew of a friend who was visiting Savannah, what he missed most about New Orleans. "Red beans and rice" was his answer. When we are far from home, what we miss most is the taste of home cookin', those familiar dishes we grew up eating. And so, in honor of all of those folks displaced from their beloved Big Easy, here's a menu to feed a crowd that will set your taste buds on fire. Have yourselves your own little Mardi Gras, no matter where you are!

Paula's Pearls of Wisdom

*In times of crisis, we are all given an opportunity
to shine, as we become our brothers' keepers.*

```
MENU
Muffuletta Sandwiches
Jambalaya
Shrimp Étouffée
Red Beans and Rice
Sweet Potato Biscuits
Mardi Gras King Cake
Krispy Kreme Bread Pudding with
Rum Sauce
French Quarter Beignets
Café au Lait
```

MUFFULETTA SANDWICHES

These are just delicious, but quite rich! The olive salad would be a great spread for French bread, too.

  Cut these into halves or quarters for a buffet.

OLIVE SALAD

¾ cup pitted green olives

⅔ cup pitted black olives

One 2½-ounce jar chopped
  pimientos, drained

3 cloves garlic

2 teaspoons anchovy paste

½ cup minced fresh parsley

1 teaspoon dried oregano

¼ teaspoon pepper

½ cup olive oil

1. In a food processor, combine the salad ingredients and pulse 4 or 5 times to roughly chop. Place in a covered container and refrigerate overnight.

2. When ready to make the sandwiches, preheat the broiler.

3. Slice the rolls horizontally and lay each open flat. Scoop out a little of the soft bread on the thicker side of the roll; be careful not to break the crust. Spoon the olive salad into the indentation. Top both halves with several slices of salami, ham, and provolone cheese. Run under the broiler until the pro-

SANDWICHES

6 individual soft French rolls

½ pound thinly sliced hard
  salami

½ pound thinly sliced ham,
  any kind

½ pound thinly sliced
  provolone cheese

volone is melted, 3 to 4 minutes. Close up the sandwiches after broiling.

Makes 6 sandwiches

JAMBALAYA

With chicken, sausage, shrimp, oysters, and *crab in it, how could this be anything but good?*

1 teaspoon salt

2 large chicken breast halves, on the bone

1½ tablespoons butter

2 cloves garlic, minced

1 cup chopped celery

1 cup chopped green bell pepper

½ cup chopped yellow onion

2 cups cooked white rice

1 pound smoked sausage, cut into 1-inch pieces, such as kielbasa

One 14.5-ounce can Creole-spiced stewed tomatoes

½ cup dry sherry

1½ pounds medium shrimp, peeled and deveined

1 cup shucked raw oysters, drained

1 cup fresh crabmeat (8 ounces), picked through twice for shells

Salt and pepper

Hot sauce (optional)

1. In a 3-quart saucepan with a lid, place 2 cups water and the salt. Bring the water to a boil, reduce the heat, and gently boil the chicken breasts until done, about 25 minutes. Allow the breasts to cool in the broth, then remove them from the liquid. Reserve the chicken broth. Shred the chicken meat and set aside.

2. In a small sauté pan, melt the butter. Sauté the garlic, celery, green pepper, and onion until the vegetables are limp, about 3 minutes. Set aside.

3. In the original 3-quart saucepan, bring the chicken broth to a boil. Add the rice and sausage. Bring back to a boil. Add the tomatoes, sautéed vegetables, shredded chicken, and sherry. Simmer for about 15 minutes.

4. Add the shrimp, oysters, and crabmeat. Cover and cook until the shrimp are pink, 5 to 8 minutes.

5. Check for seasoning and add salt and pepper to taste. Add hot sauce, if desired.

Serves 6 to 8 as a main course, or 10 to 12 as part of a buffet

SHRIMP ÉTOUFFÉE

The word étouffée *means "smothered." You start with a roux—which is just butter and flour cooked until it turns a caramel color and is used to thicken the sauce. Don't let your roux burn, or you'll have to throw it out and start from scratch. The salmon color of this dish is just beautiful served over white rice!*

6 tablespoons (¾ stick) butter

¼ cup all-purpose flour

1 cup chopped yellow onion

½ cup chopped green bell pepper

1 cup chopped celery

3 cloves garlic, finely minced

2 pounds small shrimp, peeled and deveined

½ teaspoon black pepper

½ teaspoon cayenne pepper, or to taste

1 teaspoon Cajun seasoning

⅓ cup minced green onions

⅓ cup minced fresh parsley

2 to 3 dashes of Tabasco sauce

One 14.5-ounce can diced tomatoes, with juice

1 to 2 teaspoons salt

Diced green onions, for garnish

1. Melt the butter in the bottom of a large heavy saucepan over low heat. Gradually whisk in the flour to form a paste. Continue cooking over low heat, stirring with a wooden spoon occasionally, until the mixture turns a caramel color, 15 to 20 minutes.

2. Add the onion, green pepper, celery, and garlic and cook over low heat about 5 minutes, until the vegetables are limp.

3. Add the shrimp and stir to coat in the roux. Add the black pepper, cayenne pepper, Cajun seasoning, green onions, parsley, and Tabasco to taste.

4. Add 1 cup water and stir until blended. Add the tomatoes and their juice and stir to blend. Taste for seasoning. Add the salt, starting with 1 teaspoon, then add more if needed. Bring the mixture to a boil, then reduce the heat to low and simmer for 10 to 15 minutes, until the shrimp are firm and pink and the flavors have blended.

5. Transfer the étouffée to a tureen or serving bowl. Garnish with the green onions.

Serves 6 to 8 as a main course, or 10 to 12 as part of a buffet

RED BEANS AND RICE

*R*ed beans and rice remind me of the Hoppin' John we serve on New Year's Day. The beans cook so long that they make a red "gravy" that is just delicious over rice. Of all the dishes in New Orleans, this is probably the most humble, and the one New Orleans natives love the best. (You can find jars of ham base at the supermarket.)

1 pound dried red kidney
   beans
1 large, meaty ham bone or
   ham hock, or other smoked
   meat
1½ teaspoons salt
½ teaspoon pepper
2 bay leaves
1 teaspoon hot sauce, your
   favorite brand
2 tablespoons olive oil
1 large yellow onion, minced
2 celery stalks, minced
2 cloves garlic, minced
1 tablespoon ham base, or
   1 package Goya ham-
   flavored seasoning
Canned chicken broth, as
   needed
1 pound smoked sausage, hot
   or mild, cut into 2-inch
   pieces, or andouille sausage
   (optional)
3 cups cooked white rice

1. Place the beans in a large pot and cover with water. Soak the beans overnight. Drain and rinse the beans. If you don't have time to soak the beans (or if you forgot!), rinse them and then cook about 2 hours longer than the recipe indicates, or until soft.

2. Place the beans in a large pot with a lid. Add 8 cups water, the meat, salt, pepper, bay leaves, and hot sauce; it is important to measure the water. In a large saucepan, heat the olive oil. Sauté the onion, celery, and garlic for 3 minutes until limp, then add to the beans. Turn the heat to high and bring to a boil. Add the ham base and stir well to dissolve. Cover the pot and reduce the heat to low. Simmer the beans for 2 to 2½ hours, stirring occasionally to keep the beans from sticking. It is very important to keep the temperature low so that the water doesn't cook out before the beans are done. If you must add more liquid, add a little chicken broth; if you keep adding more water, the flavor of the dish will be diluted and your seasonings will be off. Remove the ham bone when the beans are done.

3. If you are adding sausage, add it after the first 1½ hours of cooking.

4. To serve, remove the bay leaves. Place ½ cup of rice on each plate. Spoon the red beans, sausage, if using, and gravy over the rice.

Serves 6

{ Note: For best results, cook the beans a day in advance, refrigerate, and reheat. Leftovers freeze well. }

SWEET POTATO BISCUITS

I just had to come up with a biscuit to sop up all that delicious red bean gravy. These are a light orange color and delicious with plenty of soft butter!

¾ cup canned sweet potatoes, drained and mashed, then measured

4 tablespoons (½ stick) butter, softened

¼ cup sugar

2 cups all-purpose flour

2½ teaspoons baking powder

½ teaspoon baking soda

1 teaspoon salt

⅓ cup buttermilk

1. Preheat the oven to 400°F. Spray a baking sheet with vegetable oil cooking spray or line it with parchment paper.

2. In a food processor, combine the sweet potatoes, butter, and sugar and process until blended. Sift together the flour, baking powder, baking soda, and salt. Add to the sweet potato mixture and pulse until the flour mixture is evenly distributed. Add the buttermilk through the feed tube. Pulse again until the mixture forms into a ball.

3. Turn the dough ball out onto a lightly floured surface and knead several times, until the dough holds together, dusting your fingers with flour if you need to.

4. Gently roll the dough out into an 8 by 10-inch rectangle about ½ inch thick. Using a pizza cutter, cut the dough into 12 rectangular biscuits. Transfer to the baking sheet.

5. Bake in the upper third of the oven for about 10 minutes, until golden on top and the bottom has begun to turn light brown. Serve hot with butter and honey.

Makes 12 biscuits

MARDI GRAS KING CAKE

Is this a bread or a cake? You decide! This is the traditional cake eaten at Mardi Gras parties in New Orleans. Typically, a tiny plastic pink baby or an uncooked red bean is baked in the dough; whoever gets the piece with the baby or bean has to make the next cake. I do warn you, however, that the last time I made this, I cooked it with a red bean, which was swallowed by the little girl who happened to get that piece of cake! (She was fine.) The sprinkles are the traditional colors of Mardi Gras: purple, gold, and green, representing justice, power, and faith.

½ cup (1 stick) butter, softened

⅔ cup evaporated milk

¾ cup plus 1 teaspoon granulated sugar

1 teaspoon salt

2 envelopes active dry yeast, regular or rapid rise

3 eggs

Grated zest of 1 lemon

6 cups all-purpose flour

4 tablespoons (½ stick) butter, melted

1 egg white, for glazing

CINNAMON-SUGAR FILLING

½ cup granulated sugar

1 teaspoon ground cinnamon

WHITE ICING

2 cups confectioners' sugar

2 tablespoons whole milk

COLORED SUGAR

¾ cup granulated sugar

Yellow, green, red, and blue food coloring

1. Melt the butter in the microwave in a medium mixing bowl. Add the evaporated milk, ¾ cup of the sugar, and the salt. Stir so that the sugar dissolves. Allow to cool.

2. Dissolve the yeast in ¼ cup lukewarm water and stir in the remaining teaspoon sugar. Allow to stand for 10 minutes, until foamy. If the yeast does not foam up, it is no good, so you'll have to start over with new yeast and sugar.

3. Add the yeast mixture to the butter and milk mixture. Add the eggs and lemon zest and whisk together vigorously, until well blended.

4. Whisk in the flour, 1 cup at a time, until you have a thick paste—about 3 cups flour. Then switch to a wooden spoon and continue adding flour and mixing well. Do not add more than 6 cups flour, or your cake will be too dense. When you have added all the flour, turn the dough out onto a lightly floured wooden board and knead it with your hands, which you have dusted with flour, until the dough is smooth and elastic, about a dozen turns.

5. Place the dough into a large clean bowl that you have sprayed with vegetable oil cooking spray. Turn the dough to coat all sides with spray. Cover the bowl with

a tea towel and allow the dough to rise in a warm place until doubled, about 1 hour.

6. Make the cinnamon-sugar filling: Combine the sugar and cinnamon in a small dish and stir well.

7. Punch the dough down and divide the dough in two. Roll out each half into a 10 by 15-inch rectangle. Brush each rectangle with half of the melted butter and then sprinkle each rectangle with half of the cinnamon-sugar filling mixture. Roll up along the long end like a jelly roll. Press the roll together at the seam, sealing with water if necessary. Wind the two rolls together, forming one thick piece. On a baking sheet sprayed with vegetable oil cooking spray, form the dough into a circle and seal the ends together.

8. Cover with a tea towel and allow the cake to rise in a warm place for about 1 hour (when it rises, the center will close up and it will look like a bumpy "cake"), until it almost doubles in size.

9. Preheat the oven to 350°F. Whisk the egg white with 1 tablespoon water. Brush the top of the cake with the egg white. Bake the cake for 35 minutes, until it is browned and sounds hollow when tapped.

10. Make the white icing: Combine the sugar and milk in a small dish and whisk until smooth. If the mixture seems too thin, add a little more sugar. If it won't drizzle, add a little more milk, ½ teaspoon at a time.

11. Make the colored sugar: Place ¼ cup sugar in each of three custard cups. Put 1 drop of yellow food coloring into one, then, using your fingers, grind the color into the sugar until all of the granules are colored. Do the same using green food coloring, and in the third cup, blend 1 drop of red coloring and 1 drop of blue coloring to make purple.

12. Allow the cake to cool for a few minutes on a wire rack. Drizzle with icing and sprinkle the colored sugar in random patterns over the white icing. Slice across the width of the cake into thin slices to serve.

Makes about 24 thin slices

KRISPY KREME BREAD PUDDING WITH RUM SAUCE

The story behind this recipe is probably longer than the recipe itself. But all I'm going to say is that this recipe was sent to me by one of my cooking show's faithful viewers, Bill Nicholson, who lives in Florida. He created this recipe and serves it at all of his dinner parties. Lo and behold, during the filming of Paula's Cooking School, *we literally ran into Bill. I was able to have him on the show and introduce him to everybody. This is one great recipe, ya'll.*

24 Krispy Kreme glazed
   doughnuts
One 14-ounce can sweetened
   condensed milk
One 14.5-ounce can fruit
   cocktail, with juice
2 eggs, beaten
One 9-ounce box (1½ cups)
   raisins
Pinch of salt
1 teaspoon ground cinnamon

BUTTER-RUM SAUCE
½ cup (1 stick) butter
3 cups sifted confectioners'
   sugar
2 tablespoons white rum

1. Preheat the oven to 350°F. Spray a 13 by 9-inch glass dish with vegetable oil cooking spray.

2. In a very large bowl, tear or cut the doughnuts into 1-inch cubes. In another bowl, combine the condensed milk, fruit cocktail, eggs, raisins, salt, and cinnamon. Pour the mixture over the doughnuts and stir to combine. Allow the doughnuts to soak for 15 minutes. Pour the doughnut mixture into the prepared dish and press down with the back of a spoon to remove any air pockets.

3. Bake the pudding for 1 hour, until the center is firm.

4. To make the butter-rum sauce: Melt the butter in a 1-quart saucepan over low heat. Slowly stir in the sugar. Add the rum. Remove from the heat and stir well. Serve the warm sauce with the warm pudding.

Serves 12 to 16

{ Note: You can buy doughnuts from the day-old bread store to cut down on the cost. }

FRENCH QUARTER BEIGNETS

Is there anything quite like a fresh-out-of-the-deep-fryer beignet with a cup of thick chicory coffee? Kids love to shake the sugar on these, but please don't let them get close to the frying pan and the hot grease!

½ cup granulated sugar

1 envelope (1 scant tablespoon) active dry yeast

1½ teaspoons salt

2 large eggs, well beaten

1 cup evaporated milk

7 cups bread flour

¼ cup vegetable shortening

1 quart or more canola oil, for deep frying

Confectioners' sugar, for dusting

1. In a large mixing bowl, add the granulated sugar and yeast to 1½ cups lukewarm water. Allow to stand for about 10 minutes, until the mixture is very foamy.

2. Whisk in the salt, eggs, and milk. Stir well. Add 3 cups of the flour and whisk until the batter is smooth. Add the vegetable shortening and whisk until smooth. Begin adding the rest of the flour, stirring well with a wooden spoon after each ½-cup addition.

3. Turn the dough out onto a floured board and knead until smooth, about a dozen turns, adding a little more flour if necessary to keep it from sticking.

4. Spray a large clean bowl with vegetable oil cooking spray and place the dough into the bowl, turning to coat all sides. Cover the dough with plastic wrap and refrigerate for at least 2 hours or overnight.

5. When ready to make the beignets, divide the dough into 6 pieces. Roll each piece out on a slightly floured board to a 15 by 20-inch rectangle with a thickness of ½ inch. Using a pizza cutter, cut into 10 rectangles about 1½ inches wide and 2 inches long.

6. Pour the oil into a deep fryer, electric skillet, or deep frying pan. The oil should be 3 inches deep. Heat the oil to 350°F. Place 1 cup confectioners' sugar into a paper bag.

7. Drop 4 rectangles at a time into the hot oil. Brown on both sides, about 1 to 2 minutes on each side. Lift with tongs and drain on a paper towel–lined plate. Shake the warm beignets in the paper bag and

serve immediately. If necessary, add oil to keep the depth at 3 inches. Add confectioners' sugar 1 cup at a time to the shaking bag as needed.

Makes about 60 beignets

CAFÉ AU LAIT

Chicory coffee is stronger than regular coffee. You can find it on most grocery store shelves. The whipping cream lightens the strong taste. If you can't find chicory coffee, just brew a pot of good strong coffee. Chicory coffee can be ordered from Amazon.com.

FOR EACH SERVING

2 tablespoons (or more) whipping cream
1 cup hot brewed chicory coffee
Sugar cubes

Heat the cream in a small saucepan and add to the hot coffee. Add sugar to taste.

My Wedding Anniversary

I got married in Savannah's Bethesda Chapel at the Bethesda Home for Boys on the beautiful Skidaway River near Savannah, on March 6, 2004. Us second-time-arounders have to make the most of our anniversaries. Michael and I say that we have to celebrate every month if we're ever gonna make it to our fiftieth!

Michael and me on our wedding day, at Bethesda Chapel.

Paula's Pearls of Wisdom

The only things you need to make for this celebration,
girls, are your face, and reservations!

MY TURN

When you ask me "What makes a celebration?" I'd have to say any time that the family can all be together, that's a celebration. The food plays a part, certainly, but it's not the main thing. I'm a harbor pilot; my son, Anthony, works one week off and one week on on a tugboat, and my daughter, Michelle, is an RN, and then there are the two restaurants, so you can see how difficult it is for everyone to be off at the same time.

I have two brothers, and my father had three brothers, and my mother had three sisters and a brother, so I naturally had a lot of cousins. I was born and raised right on the creek where Paula and I live now, so I have lots of wonderful memories of family get-togethers, mostly holidays. The summertime was always special—there were horses and boats and motorcycles around, so it was a fun time for kids. Mama was a traditional cook, and there was always something good on the stove, usually something that had to do with fish or shrimp or crab. I could live off seafood, although I do like an occasional steak and potato.

I have a wonderful memory of my mother picking crabs while she was floating in an inner tube in the creek—she had one inner tube for herself, and put the pot of crabs in a second inner tube. She'd sun and pick crabs; I can see her right now.

If you were to ask me what my favorite meal is that Paula cooks just for me, it would have to be oxtails; we call it a swinging sirloin. I'd want them served with her green beans, fried corn, and her hoecakes. She makes so many great sweets, it would be hard to pick just one—I've got a huge sweet tooth, and she has a good time trying to fill it!

Michael Groover

DORA'S OXTAILS

Dora Charles is the head cook for the Lady & Sons Restaurant. She is a driving force behind the restaurant's success.

Dora and I have been together since my Best Western days; we are soul sisters. When I can't be at the restaurant, I don't have to worry—everybody knows that they are under Ms. Dora's watchful eye.

2 to 3 pounds oxtails
1 teaspoon House Seasoning (page 147)
1 teaspoon seasoned salt
1 large yellow onion, cut into thin strips
1 green bell pepper, cut into thin strips
3 bay leaves
½ cup Worcestershire sauce
2 tablespoons cornstarch

1. Preheat the oven to 300°F.

2. Wash the oxtails and pat dry. Season with the House Seasoning and seasoned salt. Place the oxtails in a 13 by 9-inch covered flameproof casserole. Add the onion, green pepper, bay leaves, and Worcestershire sauce. Add 1 cup water. Cover the casserole and bake for 3 to 4 hours. Check after 2½ hours; the meat is done when it begins to fall off the bone.

3. When the oxtails are done, remove them to a serving platter and keep warm. Discard the bay leaves. Mix the cornstarch with ¼ cup cold water until smooth and pour into the hot sauce. Stir to blend and pour over the oxtails. The cornstarch will thicken the sauce.

Serves 2

{ Note: When I fix these for Michael, I leave out the bell pepper and substitute soy sauce for the Worcestershire sauce. }

St. Patrick's Day

*G*rowing up in Albany, Georgia, the only thing I knew about St. Patrick's Day was that if you didn't wear green to school, you'd get pinched. When I moved to Savannah in 1987, I discovered that St. Patrick's Day was a much bigger deal; because Savannah has such a large Irish Catholic population, everybody celebrates this holiday. In fact, the Savannah celebration is second in size only to New York City's.

At one time, I lived on the parade route. I opened my home to family and friends and would feed them a St. Patrick's–style breakfast—link sausage, scrambled eggs, and green grits. My little house would be filled with guests—the balcony would be loaded, and others would be setting up their chairs on the sidewalk outside of the house to get a front-row seat for the parade. Each St. Patrick's Day brings back so many good memories!

Well, after the parade, it would be time to start on the rest of our eating frenzy, and that could be anything from lamb stew to corned beef and cabbage to Reuben sandwiches. So, whether you preferred to celebrate your St. Patrick's Day with a breakfast, a lunch, or a dinner, I think you'll really like these recipes. They certainly are very, very big in our community!

Paula's Pearls of Wisdom
I used to think people were lucky, but I've found that the harder I work, the luckier I am!

MINI REUBENS

These are delicious as an appetizer, but they also travel well if you decide to picnic. Wrap them in foil and keep warm for several hours in a small cooler with no ice.

48 slices cocktail bread—rye if
    you can find it, but white
    and pumpernickel are fine if
    you can't
Mayonnaise
Deli mustard
2 pounds deli corned beef,
    thinly sliced
Swiss cheese slices, cut to
    fit bread, approximately
    1 pound
One 15-ounce can sauerkraut,
    drained well
Melted butter

1. Spread 1 slice of bread with mayonnaise and another with deli mustard. In each sandwich, layer corned beef, Swiss cheese, and ½ tablespoon of sauerkraut. Close the sandwich.

2. Brush the butter on the outside of the sandwiches, and grill as you would if making grilled cheese sandwiches.

3. Wrap the sandwiches in foil until guests arrive, then place on a plate and pass for hors d'oeuvres.

Makes 24 sandwiches

LAMB STEW

I have never eaten or cooked much lamb, but lamb stew is just the perfect St. Patrick's Day dish for a party, so I altered one of my favorite beef stew recipes. I think you'll like the result as much as I do.

Salt and pepper

3 pounds leg of lamb meat, cut into 1½-inch cubes

¼ cup vegetable oil

¼ cup olive oil

6 celery stalks, chopped

2 large yellow onions, chopped

2 large leeks, chopped

2 cups finely chopped cabbage

½ teaspoon ground coriander

½ teaspoon ground thyme

2 cups canned beef consommé or beef broth

One 14.5-ounce can diced tomatoes, with juice

12 small new potatoes, scrubbed

Green Peas (page 70)

1. Preheat the oven to 300°F.

2. Salt and pepper the lamb chunks. In a large ovenproof Dutch oven, sauté the meat in the oils until it is browned on all sides. Remove the meat from the Dutch oven and set aside.

3. In the same Dutch oven, sauté the celery, onions, leeks, and cabbage until limp, about 3 minutes. Season with the coriander and thyme. Add the consommé and tomatoes.

4. Return the meat to the Dutch oven, cover, and bake for 1 hour.

5. Using a vegetable peeler, remove a ring of peel around the middle of the potatoes. Add the potatoes to the stew after an hour. Cook the stew for another hour, or until the meat is fork-tender.

6. Serve the stew with a side dish of green peas.

Serves 8 to 10

GREEN PEAS

Don't laugh. My family loves these as much as anything fresh I make.

Two 14.5-ounce cans LeSueur
   peas, well drained
4 tablespoons (½ stick) butter
Salt and pepper

Heat the peas in a medium saucepan with the butter for about 3 minutes, until just heated through. Add salt and pepper to taste.

Serves 8

PARMESAN SCONES

Okay, so scones are Scottish. They are also a cousin of our southern buttermilk biscuits, and they go great with the lamb stew. We threw in the Parmesan cheese for flavor—sort of a Scottish cheese biscuit!

2 cups all-purpose flour
1 tablespoon baking powder
½ teaspoon salt
⅓ cup freshly grated Parmesan cheese, plus a little more for sprinkling
½ cup (1 stick) butter, cut into cubes and softened
1 egg, beaten
½ cup whole milk
2 tablespoons (¼ stick) butter, melted

1. Preheat the oven to 400°F.

2. In a food processor fitted with the steel blade, combine the flour, baking powder, salt, and Parmesan and pulse three times or until blended. Add the butter to the dry mixture. Turn the machine on for 45 seconds, until the butter is blended with the dry ingredients.

3. Transfer the mixture to a medium mixing bowl. In a small bowl, combine the egg and milk and pour at once into the flour mixture. With a fork, gently mix until the dough sticks together. It will be rather wet.

4. Turn the dough onto a floured board and, with floured hands, gently knead three times, until the dough holds together. The dough will be moist. Pat the dough out to a ½-inch thickness. Cut with a 1- to 1½-inch biscuit cutter. Place the scones onto an ungreased baking sheet. Brush the tops with the melted butter and sprinkle each with a pinch or two of Parmesan cheese. You may reroll any leftover dough.

5. Bake for 11 to 13 minutes, until golden brown. Serve warm with butter.

Makes about 12 scones

GREEN GRITS PIE

There are a few recipes that have become a part of who I am and this is one of them. I can't tell you how many times I've served this pie. It's always a surprise to the people who are lucky enough to have a piece—they just can't believe the filling is made with our good ol' southern grits! The grits give this a taste very similar to chess pie, which is made with cornmeal.

⅛ teaspoon salt

¼ cup quick-cooking grits (not instant)

½ cup (1 stick) butter

Green food coloring

¾ cup sugar

2 tablespoons all-purpose flour

3 large eggs, lightly beaten

¼ cup buttermilk

1 teaspoon vanilla extract

One 9-inch frozen piecrust, thawed, or 1 refrigerated piecrust, unbaked, fitted into a 9-inch glass pie plate

1 cup whipping cream, whipped and sweetened with 1 tablespoon confectioners' sugar and colored with 1 drop of green food coloring

Strawberries, for garnish

1. Preheat the oven to 325°F.

2. In a small saucepan, bring ¾ cup water and the salt to a boil. Add the grits, reduce the heat, cover, and cook over low heat for 5 minutes, stirring several times, until the grits are very thick. Add the butter and 1 drop of food coloring and stir until the butter melts. Set the grits aside and allow them to cool slightly.

3. In a small bowl, stir together the sugar, flour, eggs, buttermilk, and vanilla. Stir well into the cooled grits. Pour the mixture into the piecrust. Bake for 35 to 40 minutes, until set.

4. Serve warm or cold with whipped cream, and garnish with strawberries.

Serves 8

CRÈME DE MENTHE BROWNIES

These are a staple at Savannah St. Pat's parties. And no wonder. They look beautiful and taste delicious!

4 ounces (4 squares) unsweetened baking chocolate

1 cup (2 sticks) butter

4 large eggs

2 cups granulated sugar

½ teaspoon salt

1 teaspoon vanilla extract

1 cup all-purpose flour

FILLING

½ cup (1 stick) butter, softened

2 cups sifted confectioners' sugar

4 tablespoons green crème de menthe

ICING

6 ounces (1 cup) semisweet chocolate chips

6 tablespoons (¾ stick) butter

1. Preheat the oven to 350°F. Spray a 13 by 9-inch baking pan with vegetable oil cooking spray.

2. In a double boiler, melt the chocolate and butter over simmering water. Cool slightly.

3. In a medium mixing bowl, beat the eggs with a whisk until blended, then add the sugar and continue whisking until the mixture is light and fluffy. Add the cooled chocolate mixture, the salt, vanilla, and flour. Beat with the whisk until all of the ingredients are thoroughly blended.

4. Pour the batter into the prepared pan. Bake for 25 minutes. Cool in the pan.

5. Make the filling: With an electric mixer, beat together the butter and sugar until well blended. Stir in the crème de menthe. Blend well. Spread over the cooled brownies. Refrigerate in the original baking pan until the filling is firm.

6. Make the icing: Melt the chocolate chips and butter in the top of a double boiler. Stir until smooth. Pour the warm glaze over the filling. Tilt the pan to ice the filling evenly. Refrigerate until the chocolate hardens.

7. To cut the brownies, remove the pan from the refrigerator and allow the brownies to come to room temperature so the chocolate will not crack. Cut into 48 brownies. Remove the brownies from the pan and store in the refrigerator in an airtight container.

Makes 48 brownies

❖ BRANDON'S DECORATING TIPS ❖

Take potted shamrocks out of their containers and pot them in cups
and saucers. Place them down the center of the table. Hollow out limes
and use them for tea light holders, or you can also shave the bottom
off the limes so they will sit flat, then make a little slit in the top
and use them for place card holders.

Easter Dinner

*W*hen I was growing up, I went to regular church services with my family. For Easter I always had a new bonnet and a fancy new outfit. Mama would be rushing around, trying to finish the Easter meal, which always featured ham.

After I married and had children, my favorite way to spend Easter was to attend sunrise services, take the children to breakfast, and come back home so that they could see if the Easter bunny had come. They could enjoy their baskets and I could take the opportunity to slip back into bed!

Now that I'm in the restaurant business, I'm back to cooking the traditional Easter meal for my restaurant guests, and it still stars ham!

Like having a big turkey at Thanksgiving, one of the best things about ham is the leftovers. I do love ham salad, and I've included one of my favorite recipes.

My parents, little brother Bubba, and me.

Paula's Pearls of Wisdom

Easter is the celebration of rebirth, a new day, a new start, the opportunity to make right any of our wrongs.

PEANUT BUTTER–GLAZED HAM

Cooking a ham is easy if you start with premium meat. Ham goes well with any number of glazes, but this one is really yummy with the saltiness of the ham. You can use it over grilled ham slices, too.

One 10- to 12-pound whole
    smoked picnic ham, rinsed
    and patted dry, untrimmed
1 cup chicken broth
½ cup creamy peanut butter
¼ cup honey
1 clove garlic, chopped
2 teaspoons soy sauce

1. Position an oven rack in the lower third of your oven. Preheat the oven to 325°F.

2. Place the ham on a rack in a roasting pan. Place the pan in the oven and roast the ham for 20 minutes per pound. If the ham begins to burn, cover loosely with foil.

3. At the end of the cooking time, in a blender or food processor, combine the broth, peanut butter, honey, garlic, and soy sauce. Slather the glaze all over the surface of the ham and cook an additional 20 minutes.

4. Remove the ham from the oven and allow it to sit for about 15 minutes before carving.

Serve 12 to 14

SUCCOTASH

Succotash is just fresh corn off-the-cob and baby butter beans or lima beans. What could be better? If you are lucky enough to get farm-fresh produce, then you will have the best ingredients. However, this dish is almost as good when you use frozen baby butter or lima beans and corn, or supermarket corn that you cut off the cob. The name succotash comes from an Indian word meaning "boiled corn."

½ teaspoon House Seasoning
  (page 147)
½ teaspoon seasoned salt
1 chicken bouillon cube or
  1 teaspoon granulated
  bouillon
One 10-ounce package frozen
  baby butter beans or lima
  beans
6 slices bacon, cut into tiny
  pieces
3 ears fresh corn, kernels cut
  from cob, or one 10-ounce
  package frozen corn kernels
2 tablespoons (¼ stick) butter
¼ teaspoon pepper

1. In a medium saucepan, add the House Seasoning, seasoned salt, and bouillon cube to 2 cups water. Add the butter beans or lima beans and bring to a boil. Reduce the heat, cover, and cook over low heat for about 20 minutes, until the butter beans are tender and some of the water has been absorbed.

2. In a medium skillet, sauté the bacon until it is very crisp.

3. Drain off all except 1 tablespoon grease. Add the corn to the skillet with the bacon pieces and cook over medium-low heat for about 10 minutes. Using a slotted spoon, add the butter beans to the skillet. Add a little of the butter bean liquid to create a sauce. Add the butter and pepper. Stir well and serve.

Serves 8 to 10

SPINACH-SWISS CASSEROLE

Is this a spinach soufflé or a casserole? Who cares, when it tastes so good? You can serve it hot or at room temperature, and I think it makes a nice brunch or lunch dish, too.
Baking the soufflé in a hot-water bath will give the dish a silky texture.

One 10-ounce package frozen
    chopped spinach
¼ cup finely minced yellow
    onion
4 tablespoons (½ stick) butter
3 tablespoons all-purpose flour
½ teaspoon salt
Pinch of cayenne pepper
¼ teaspoon black pepper
1 cup whole milk
1 cup (¼ pound) grated Swiss
    cheese
½ cup freshly grated Parmesan
    cheese
3 eggs, beaten well

1. Preheat the oven to 325°F. Spray a 1½-quart casserole with vegetable oil cooking spray.

2. Remove the spinach from the packaging and transfer to a microwave-safe bowl. Microwave on high for 2 minutes. Remove the spinach and squeeze dry with your hands. Place the spinach into a medium mixing bowl.

3. In a skillet, over medium-low heat, sauté the onion in 1 tablespoon of the butter until soft, about 3 to 4 minutes. Add the onion to the spinach.

4. In the same skillet, melt the remaining 3 tablespoons butter over medium-low heat. Whisk in the flour, salt, cayenne pepper, and black pepper. Stir until smooth. Slowly add the milk and continue stirring until the mixture thickens, 3 to 5 minutes. Turn off the heat. Stir in the Swiss and Parmesan cheeses and continue stirring until the mixture is smooth. Pour the sauce over the spinach in the mixing bowl. Add the eggs and stir well.

5. Pour the spinach mixture into the casserole. Place the casserole into a larger casserole filled with 1 inch of water (a hot-water bath) and bake for 45 minutes.

Serves 8 to 10

SQUASH BOATS

I'm not sure that there's any way to improve upon a good squash casserole, but these squash boats are fun and different and will please the little ones at your Easter table.

4 medium yellow squash or
    zucchini
2 tablespoons (¼ stick) butter
1 small yellow onion, finely
    chopped
½ teaspoon salt
¼ teaspoon pepper
2 saltine crackers, crushed
    into crumbs
1 cup (¼ pound) shredded
    sharp Cheddar cheese

1. Preheat the oven to 350°F. Lightly butter a baking dish large enough to hold the squash on a small rimmed baking sheet.

2. Boil the whole squash in a medium saucepan in about 2 cups water over medium heat until the squash are tender, about 15 minutes.

3. Remove the squash from the water, drain, and allow to cool. Cut the squash in half lengthwise. Using a small spoon, gently scoop out the pulp, leaving the shape of the squash intact. Place the squash shells in the prepared dish.

4. In a small skillet, melt the butter and sauté the onion until tender, about 3 to 5 minutes. Add the salt and pepper. Add the squash pulp and cracker crumbs. Stuff the filling into the squash shells. Top each squash boat with enough cheese to cover the filling.

5. Bake for 20 minutes. Serve hot or at room temperature.

Serves 8

BUTTERHORNS

These yeasty, buttery light rolls are gorgeous to look at and easy to eat.

1 package (1 scant
    tablespoon) active dry yeast
½ cup plus 1 teaspoon sugar
½ cup (1 stick) butter, melted
3 eggs, beaten
4 cups all-purpose flour
1 teaspoon salt
Butter, softened

1. In a small glass dish, add the yeast and 1 teaspoon of the sugar to 1 cup lukewarm water. Allow the mixture to sit until the yeast begins to bubble, about 10 minutes.

2. In a medium mixing bowl, combine the butter, the remaining ½ cup sugar, and the eggs. Add the yeast mixture and stir well. Sift together the flour and salt. Add the flour to the yeast mixture and stir well. Place the dough into a large greased bowl and turn the dough to grease all sides. Cover with plastic wrap and refrigerate the dough overnight.

3. Punch the dough down and divide in half with a sharp knife. On a heavily floured surface, roll out half the dough into a large circle about ¼ inch thick. Using a pizza cutter, cut the dough into 16 wedges. Roll up each wedge from wide end to the tip, making a crescent. Repeat with the other half of the dough. Place each roll onto a baking sheet lined with parchment paper and cover with a clean, lightweight tea towel. Allow to rise in a warm place for about 1 hour, until doubled in size.

4. Preheat the oven to 375°F.

5. Bake the rolls for 10 to 12 minutes, until lightly browned.

6. Rub the tops of the rolls with softened butter immediately after they come out of the oven. Serve warm.

Makes 32 rolls

{ Note: The rolls may also be underbaked (tops will just begin to brown), allowed to cool completely, then stored in the freezer in resealable plastic bags. When ready to serve, thaw for about 30 minutes at room temperature. Reheat for 3 minutes at 350°F. }

CARROT CAKE

What could be more appropriate at Easter than carrot cake for all those somebunnies you love! This dense, sweet cake is delicious, and the icing is downright addictive.

2 cups granulated sugar

1½ cups vegetable oil

4 eggs

2 cups all-purpose flour

2 teaspoons ground cinnamon

2 teaspoons baking powder

2 teaspoons baking soda

1 teaspoon salt

2 cups shredded carrots, about
    4 medium carrots

¼ cup chopped walnuts

ICING

½ cup (1 stick) butter, softened

3 cups confectioners' sugar

One 8-ounce package cream
    cheese, softened

¼ cup chopped walnuts

1. Preheat the oven to 350°F. Spray a 13 by 9-inch baking pan with vegetable oil cooking spray and dust with flour.

2. In the bowl of an electric mixer, combine the sugar, oil, and eggs. Mix at medium speed until smooth.

3. Sift together the flour, cinnamon, baking powder, baking soda, and salt. Add the flour mixture to the egg mixture and combine at low speed until smooth. With a spoon, stir in the carrots and walnuts.

4. Place the batter in the prepared pan and place on the middle rack in the oven. Bake for 50 minutes, or until a toothpick inserted in the cake comes out clean and the top of the cake springs back when touched. When the cake is done, remove from the oven and allow to cool on the countertop for 15 minutes before icing.

5. To make the icing: Beat the butter, sugar, and cream cheese in a medium bowl until smooth. Stir in the walnuts. Ice the cake when it is warm, not hot; this improves the icing's spreadability. The icing will firm up in the refrigerator. Keep the cake cold until ready to serve.

Serves 12 to 16, depending on the size of the pieces.
(It's very rich!)

HAM SALAD

I have never baked a ham and not had leftovers. Choose some kind soul who doesn't cook but likes to help to pick all of the fat and gristle from the meat and remove the ham from the bone for you. Store the meat in a resealable plastic bag until you have time to make this wonderful ham salad. Serve it in sandwiches, or all by itself with good crackers. I just love dill pickles in cold salads.

3 cups ground cooked ham
1 teaspoon Dijon mustard
¼ cup mayonnaise
2 tablespoons chopped sweet
    pickle
2 tablespoons chopped dill
    pickle
2 hard-boiled eggs, peeled
    and grated
Salt and pepper

Combine all of the ingredients gently but thoroughly. Store in a covered container in the refrigerator for up to 3 days.

Makes about 3½ cups

❖ BRANDON'S DECORATING TIPS ❖

You are going to think I've gone over the edge on this one, but here goes:
Cover the dining room table with plastic, and then line the table with sod
and hide Easter eggs in the grass. Use spring flowers: tulips, daffodils,
and hyacinths either in vases or as forced bulbs in pots.
If you don't feel up to planting your dining room table,
you could use the same idea on a sideboard or serving table.

Fried Peanut Butter and Banana Sandwich (page 31)

Crab and Spinach Casserole (page 8); Baked Tomatoes (page 9);
Blueberry Gems (page 11)

Mardi Gras King Cake (page 57)

Clockwise from right: Herb Butter (page 201), Orange-Ginger Butter (page 200),
Cinnamon-Honey Butter (page 200)

White Cake with Strawberry Icing (page 99);
Strawberries Dipped in White Chocolate (page 98)

Standing Rib Roast (page 207); Twice-Baked Potato Casserole (page 209);
Brussels Sprouts with Onion and Bacon (page 210)

The Lady & Sons Crab-Stuffed Shrimp (page 34)

Peanut Butter–Glazed Ham (page 77); Squash Boats (page 80);
Butterhorns (page 81); Succotash (page 78)

An Easter Egg Hunt

*W*hen my children were small, we always went to Easter egg hunts in Albany. And I always did my own Easter egg hunt in our yard on Easter afternoon. I can remember clapping my hands and saying, "You're getting warmer . . . warmer . . . hotter . . . you're *on fire*!" The boys had so much fun!

I am really the queen of Easter baskets. I can say that because the Queen Mother, Aunt Peggy, taught me how to make them. She and my Uncle George owned the Toy House in Albany, and before the big chains, everybody shopped at the Toy House, and Aunt Peggy made all their Easter baskets. She used to make my children's, and then one year I said, "Teach me how to do it." It's really an art form. My son Bobby said Easter was like a miniature Christmas! I went for big baskets and always tried to fill them with unexpected things, taped strategically so that they would be just where I wanted them—underwear, or a special shirt, or a baseball glove, or a baseball, or a yo-yo—whatever the boys were into at the time. They would also be loaded with candy! Then I'd cover the whole thing in clear wrap and tie it with ribbons. They'd just be beautiful—too pretty to open up!

The first year Michael and I were together, in 2001, I had a feeling that Michelle and Anthony had never gotten baskets like the ones my boys had. It was real important to me that they have ones just like the ones my children had been receiving for years. So I made them Easter baskets . . . and they just loved them, too!

We don't have Easter egg hunts anymore, but there might be some little ones around my house sometime soon, so I can get back to hiding them eggs!

Paula's Pearls of Wisdom
*Life is like an Easter egg hunt—stay
focused and the golden egg may be yours!*

PHYLLO CUPS FILLED WITH CHICKEN SALAD

This is one of the recipes I used to serve during my Bag Lady days, my first catering experience. It's still a favorite of my family and friends. You can use poached or roasted chicken.

2 tablespoons fresh lemon
    juice
½ cup mayonnaise
1 teaspoon salt
3½ cups finely diced cooked
    chicken
1 cup finely diced celery
⅓ cup slivered almonds
One 15-count package frozen
    mini phyllo (filo) shells,
    thawed

In a small bowl, combine the lemon juice, mayonnaise, and salt. Toss with the chicken, celery, and almonds in a medium bowl. Spoon into the phyllo shells; fill just before serving.

Makes 15 phyllo cups, with leftovers

PHYLLO CUPS FILLED WITH SHRIMP SALAD

This is a very simple shrimp salad—you don't want to overpower the delicate flavor of the shrimp with a strong dressing.

2 cups shrimp, cooked, peeled, and finely diced, about 1 pound

½ cup finely diced celery

1 tablespoon minced green onion

1½ tablespoons fresh lemon juice

½ cup mayonnaise

½ teaspoon salt

¼ teaspoon pepper

One 15-count package frozen mini phyllo (filo) shells, thawed

Combine the shrimp, celery, and green onion in a medium bowl. In a small bowl, stir together the lemon juice, mayonnaise, salt, and pepper. Pour over the shrimp and stir gently to combine. Spoon into the phyllo shells; fill just before serving.

Makes 15 phyllo cups, with leftovers

ASPARAGUS WITH CURRY DIP

Your young guests may not appreciate this spring dish, but your older guests certainly will.

2 pounds fresh asparagus
1 teaspoon salt
1 cup mayonnaise
1 teaspoon curry powder
1 tablespoon fresh lemon juice

1. Lay the asparagus on a cutting board and line up the tips, then cut off the bottoms evenly with a large sharp knife and discard. Fill a large skillet with about 2 inches of water. Add the salt and bring to a boil. Add the asparagus all at once and cook for about 3 minutes, until the spears are tender but still have texture. Drain immediately, roll in a tea towel, and store in the refrigerator until party time.

2. Make the curry dip: Stir together the mayonnaise, curry powder, and lemon juice in a small glass bowl. Cover with plastic wrap and keep chilled until party time.

3. Serve chilled asparagus with the curry dip.

Serves 8 to 10

SAUSAGE BISCUITS

This is such an easy way to make sausage biscuits. The biscuits curl up around the sausage during baking.

1 can refrigerator biscuits
(10 biscuits per can)
1 pound bulk sausage, formed
into 20 small flat patties
about the diameter of a
quarter, cooked and
drained
Orange marmalade

1. Preheat the oven to 375°F. Spray 20 muffin tin cups with vegetable oil cooking spray.

2. Remove the biscuits from the package and separate each one into round halves. Place the halves into the muffin cups. Press 1 sausage patty into each biscuit, pressing down so that the biscuit comes up around the edges of the sausage.

3. Bake for 10 minutes. Remove the biscuits from the tins and place on a serving platter. Serve warm with orange marmalade.

Makes 20 biscuits

DEVILED EGGS

*W*hat tastes better than a deviled egg? No picnic is complete without them. For picnics, I put the two halves together, wrap them in plastic wrap, and keep them in a container in the cooler. That way, the tops don't get messed up.

12 hard-boiled eggs
¼ cup mayonnaise
1 tablespoon diced dill pickle,
   with juice
½ teaspoon Dijon mustard
Salt and pepper
Fresh dill, for garnish

1. Peel the eggs and cut them in half lengthwise. Remove the yolks and mash them in a medium bowl. Stir in the mayonnaise, dill pickle and juice, and mustard. Taste, then add salt and pepper as needed.

2. Spoon or pipe the filling into the eggs. Place a paper towel in the bottom of a plastic container with a lid. Position the eggs close together in the container so they will not tip over. Refrigerate until serving time.

3. Serve the eggs in an old-fashioned egg dish if you have one. If not, make a bed of "grass" with the dill on a platter and put the eggs on this to keep them from sliding around.

Makes 24

CREAM CHEESE–STUFFED NEW POTATOES

I've been serving these for years at my catering events to rave reviews. You may also cut the potatoes in half and place cut side down and stuff the tops.

24 bite-size new potatoes, scrubbed, with a tiny sliver cut off each potato so they will stand after filling

One 5-ounce package Boursin cheese

4 tablespoons (½ stick) butter, softened

⅓ cup whipping cream

Salt and pepper

Finely chopped fresh parsley

Red caviar, for garnish (optional)

1. In a large pot with plenty of salted water, boil the potatoes until they are tender when a fork is inserted, about 10 to 12 minutes. Drain and let the potatoes cool until you can handle them.

2. With a melon baller, remove a scoop from each potato. Combine the Boursin, butter, and cream. Taste, and add salt and pepper as needed. Spoon or pipe the cheese mixture into the potatoes. Garnish with a fine sprinkling of parsley. Add a tiny dollop of red caviar to carry out your egg theme, if you wish! Stand the potatoes on a platter to serve.

Makes 24

{ Notes: You can make hash browns by browning the scooped-out potato in vegetable oil with plenty of onion, salt, and pepper.
If you have any of the cheese mixture left, it makes a great baked potato topping. }

MISS HELEN'S EASTER EGGS

This recipe first appeared in The Lady & Sons Just Desserts. *I prepared them in the winter of 2006 for my new magazine,* Cooking with Paula Deen, *which debuted in November 2005, and was thrilled with how adorable they were. They would just look precious on your children's table.*

2 medium white potatoes,
    peeled and diced
½ cup (1 stick) butter, sliced
Two 1-pound boxes
    confectioners' sugar, sifted
1½ teaspoons vanilla extract
8 ounces (8 squares) bitter-
    sweet chocolate

DECORATIVE ICING

1 cup vegetable shortening
4 tablespoons (½ stick) butter,
    softened
3 cups sifted confectioners'
    sugar
1½ teaspoons vanilla extract
⅛ teaspoon salt
Food coloring

1. Boil the potatoes in water to cover until they are very soft, 15 to 20 minutes. Drain and mash. Measure out ½ cup of the potatoes into a bowl. Add the butter to the potatoes while they are hot and blend well. Allow the mixture to cool.

2. Add the sugar and vanilla to the cooled potatoes. Knead the mixture by hand until it is smooth. Mold the mixture into "eggs," varying the sizes, until you have used all of the mixture. Refrigerate the eggs for 1 hour.

3. Place a wire rack over a baking sheet. Melt the chocolate in the top of a double boiler over simmering water or for 1 minute on full power in the microwave. Cool slightly. Using a slotted spoon, dip each egg into the chocolate, coating the entire egg. Place the eggs on the rack to drain, then transfer to waxed paper to harden, which will take several hours.

4. To make the decorative icing: In a large mixing bowl, beat the shortening and butter with an electric mixer until they are well blended. Add the sugar, vanilla, and salt. Beat until smooth. Divide the icing among as many bowls as you want colors. Add 1 drop of food coloring to each bowl. Decorate the eggs with the icing using pastry bags and various tips. Store the eggs in empty egg cartons in the refrigerator. It will take several hours for the decorative icing to "set up."

To serve, you can slice the eggs into thin rounds about ⅛ inch thick. They are *very* sweet.

Makes about 16 eggs, depending on size

Variation:
You can knead in any of the following to the potato mixture:
½ cup chopped nuts
½ cup flaked coconut
¼ cup chunky or creamy peanut butter

PETITS FOURS

One 1-pound loaf pound cake,
  top crust removed, cut into
  1½-inch cubes
1 teaspoon unflavored gelatin
Two 1-pound boxes
  confectioners' sugar, sifted
1 egg white
1 tablespoon light corn syrup
Food coloring

1. Arrange the pound cake cubes in a single layer on a baking sheet. Freeze until firm, 4 hours or overnight.

2. In the top of a double boiler, dissolve the gelatin in ⅔ cup cold water. Add the sugar, egg white, and corn syrup and whisk until well blended. Place over simmering water and heat to 110°F (warm to the touch). Stir well to make sure the gelatin is completely dissolved. Divide the icing among several bowls and add 1 drop of food coloring to each to tint.

3. Line a baking sheet with waxed paper. Spoon the icing over the frozen cake cubes to cover completely. Place on the prepared baking sheet and allow them to dry completely.

Makes 42 petits fours

❖ BRANDON'S DECORATING TIPS ❖

Paula takes Easter baskets and lines them with grasses and greenery and fills them with all kinds of eggs—dyed eggs and plastic eggs filled with candy and money! She uses the baskets as centerpieces.

May Day Pink and White Party

*L*ife's simple pleasures can make such wonderful memories. In Albany, Geor-gia, where I grew up, May Day meant that our middle school had game day and the crowning of the May Day Queen and her court! I loved the races—the 50-yard and 100-yard dashes, and the relay races. One May Day, I wasn't the queen, but the runner-up! The queen and her court got to wear long gowns, and we were intro-duced to the student body in the Mills Memorial Stadium. What fun that was! Believe it or not, May Day is still celebrated in Savannah by the second-graders in front of the Massie School in downtown Savannah. The children dress up and dance around the Maypole and eat a menu that is all pink and white, the traditional May Day colors.

Princess Paula.

Paula's Pearls of Wisdom

Treasure today's moments

because they will be tomorrow's memories.

CREAM CHEESE AND CHERRY SANDWICHES

One 8-ounce package cream cheese, softened

One 6-ounce jar maraschino cherries, drained but not rinsed, stems discarded, and diced

One 1-pound loaf thin-sliced white bread (store brand or Pepperidge Farm)

Combine the cream cheese and cherries. The juice that clings to the cherries will tint the cream cheese a light pink. Spread the mixture thickly on a slice of bread and then top with another slice of bread. Trim the crusts and cut into fingers or shapes, if desired. Store in airtight containers in the refrigerator until party time.

Makes 18 to 20 small sandwiches

STRAWBERRIES DIPPED IN WHITE CHOCOLATE

If you want to be extra-fancy, you can decorate the finished berries with drizzles of melted dark chocolate.

1 pint strawberries
Three 1-ounce squares white
  baking chocolate

Rinse, but do not hull, the strawberries. Drain and pat completely dry. Melt the chocolate in a glass dish in the microwave on high (100%) power for 60 seconds. Remove, stir, and microwave for 10 seconds more until the chocolate has melted. Allow the chocolate to cool slightly to thicken. Dip the bottom half of each strawberry in the melted chocolate. Twist the strawberry so that the chocolate forms a "tail" at the end. Place on waxed paper to harden.

Makes about 24 strawberries

PRETZELS DIPPED IN WHITE CHOCOLATE

Eight 1-ounce squares white
  baking chocolate
One 10-ounce bag pretzel
  rods
Pink sprinkles

Melt the chocolate in a glass dish in the microwave on high (100%) power for 60 seconds. Remove, stir, and microwave for 10 seconds more until the chocolate has melted. Continue heating in 10-second bursts until all the chocolate is melted. Allow the chocolate to cool slightly to thicken. Dip the bottom half of each pretzel rod in the melted chocolate. Twist the rod so that the chocolate forms a "tail" at the end. Over a paper plate, sprinkle the warm chocolate with pink sprinkles. Place on waxed paper to harden.

Makes about 24 pretzels

WHITE CAKE WITH STRAWBERRY ICING

This simple cake has become a family favorite. It looks, tastes, and smells like spring!

One 18.25-ounce package
   white cake mix
½ cup (1 stick) butter, softened
3 large eggs

ICING

4 tablespoons (½ stick)
   unsalted butter, softened
4 cups sifted confectioners'
   sugar, about 1 pound
6 ripe strawberries, hulled and
   mashed
6 whole strawberries, for
   garnish

1. Preheat the oven to 375°F. Grease and flour a 13 by 9-inch baking pan.

2. Blend the cake mix, ⅔ cup water, the butter, and the eggs in a large bowl with an electric mixer until well blended, about 3 minutes.

3. Pour the batter into the pan and bake for 28 to 30 minutes, until the center of the cake springs back when pressed. Cool in the pan on a wire rack for about 15 minutes.

4. Make the icing: Place the butter and 2 cups of the sugar in the bowl of an electric mixer. Beat at low speed until blended. Add the mashed strawberries and mix at medium speed until well combined. Add the remaining 2 cups sugar and beat until creamy and smooth. The icing should be thick enough to stand up on a spoon. If too thin, add more confectioners' sugar. If too thick, add a teaspoon or two of milk.

5. Frost the cooled cake in the pan. For decorative effect, make swirls in the frosting with a clean spatula. Garnish with the whole strawberries. Cut into 12 to 16 pieces, and store, covered, in the refrigerator for up to 5 days.

Serves 12 to 16

SPINACH AND STRAWBERRY SALAD

This salad was the hit at a church covered dish, and I knew I wanted to share the recipe.

One 10- to 12-ounce package
  baby spinach, washed and
  dried
¼ cup sliced almonds, toasted
1 pint strawberries, hulled and
  quartered
½ medium cucumber, peeled,
  seeded, and finely diced

DRESSING
1 tablespoon fresh lemon juice
2 tablespoons white wine
  vinegar
⅓ cup sugar
1 tablespoon vegetable oil
1 teaspoon poppy seeds

1. In a large salad bowl, toss together the spinach, almonds, strawberries, and cucumber. In a small glass dish or jar with a tight-fitting lid, combine the lemon juice, vinegar, sugar, oil, and poppy seeds. Whisk in the glass dish or shake if using a jar.

2. Dress the salad right before serving.

Serves 8 to 10

APPLE, CRANBERRY, AND WALNUT SALAD

Here's an update on the classic Waldorf salad.

2 large red apples, unpeeled, diced

2 celery stalks, diced

½ cup sweetened dried cranberries

½ cup chopped walnuts

½ cup mayonnaise

Combine all of the ingredients in a medium bowl. Stir gently with a large spoon to mix. Keep refrigerated until serving time.

Serves 4 to 6

APPLE CHICKEN SALAD WITH RED GRAPES

Chicken with fruit and nuts makes a delicious combination.

2 cups cubed cooked chicken breast meat, roasted or boiled (about 2 skinless, boneless breasts)

1 cup red grapes, halved

1 red apple, unpeeled, finely diced

One 2-ounce package slivered almonds, toasted

½ cup chopped celery

DRESSING

½ cup mayonnaise

1 tablespoon honey

1 tablespoon fresh lemon juice

½ teaspoon celery salt

Combine the chicken, grapes, apple, almonds, and celery in a medium bowl. Combine the mayonnaise, honey, lemon juice, and celery salt in a small bowl. Whisk to combine. Toss the dressing with the salad ingredients. Chill until serving time.

Serves 8 to 10

YOGURT SMOOTHIES

Even your youngest cooks can make these. They are a little tart, but beautiful and nutritious—great for breakfast!

One 32-ounce container
vanilla yogurt
One 10-ounce package frozen
sweetened strawberries,
thawed

Place the yogurt and strawberries in a blender. Whirl until smooth. Serve immediately in 6-ounce juice glasses.

Makes 6 to 8 servings

❖ BRANDON'S DECORATING TIPS ❖

Pink and white carnation topiaries look and smell beautiful.
You can get oasis topiaries at a craft store. Soak them in water,
then cut the stems of the carnations about 1½ inches long and stick them
in the oasis to cover the form. Use lots of sheer pink and white ribbons,
attached with U-shaped floral pins, and leave them long,
as if you would braid them around the Maypole.

MAMA'S GOULASH

People ask me daily what my favorite meal is, expecting they already know the answer. While I love meat and 'taters, and all the traditional southern staples, my favorite meal isn't fried chicken, collards, and corn bread, though everyone always expects me to say so. Lots of people don't know my mom's range in cooking. She is the soul food queen, but she can really lay out a spread of any kind. My mom makes a mean stir-fry, or sauerkraut and kielbasa, for that matter. And Mexican? "¡Hola, ya'll!"

Anyhow, people usually are surprised when I say, "The goulash my mama makes for my birthday every year is my favorite meal." "Goulash? What in the world . . . !" they say. Yup, my favorite thing Paula Deen makes is basically glorified Beefaroni. I would describe it as a thick, almost spaghetti sauce, chock-full of elbow macaroni and lean ground beef. If you asked my mom for the recipe, I suspect you'd get a laugh. I have never seen my mom use a recipe for her goulash, and I've never tried to re-create it at home because it is just such a wonderful, homemade, pinch-and-dash kind of meal.

I have it only once a year, and that's what makes it such a wonderful family tradition. You know, now that I'm in my mid-thirties, birthdays aren't what they once were. Don't get me wrong—I feel blessed with every passing day, and I definitely celebrate, but for different reasons. I look forward to that meal now because I know I get some alone time with my family, which is so precious; my favorite meal comes with the guarantee that I get to spend time with my family with little fanfare. I know the only camera there will be my own. (I never thought I'd be saying that!) Having a great home-cooked dish with your family is totally underrated.

Bobby Deen

Bobby's birthday party.

BOBBY'S GOULASH

2 pounds lean ground beef

1 pound ground turkey

2 large yellow onions, chopped

Two 15-ounce cans tomato sauce

Two 15-ounce cans diced tomatoes

3 cloves garlic, chopped

2 tablespoons Italian seasoning

3 bay leaves

3 tablespoons soy sauce

1 tablespoon House Seasoning (page 147)

1 tablespoon seasoned salt

2 cups elbow macaroni (uncooked)

1. In a Dutch oven, sauté the ground beef and ground turkey over medium-high heat until no pink remains. Break up the meat while sautéing. Spoon off any grease. Add the onions to the pot and sauté until they are tender, about 5 minutes. Add 3 cups water, along with the tomato sauce, tomatoes, garlic, Italian seasoning, bay leaves, soy sauce, House Seasoning, and seasoned salt. Stir well. Place a lid on the pot and allow this to cook for 15 to 20 minutes.

2. Add the elbow macaroni, stir well, return the lid to the pot, and simmer for about 30 minutes. Turn off the heat, remove the bay leaves, and allow the mixture to sit about 30 minutes more before serving.

3. Serve with garlic bread and a salad.

Serves 6, unless Bobby's eating—then it serves about 3

Cinco de Mayo Fiesta

My kids love Mexican food. Savannah has quite a large Mexican population, and we've got some pretty good Mexican restaurants here. The limit to my Mexican cooking has been tacos and beans, but I'm branching out! People think I'm "just a southern cook," and while I take that as a supreme compliment, I do like to try new things.

Cinco de Mayo literally means "Fifth of May," and the holiday commemorates the victory of the Mexican army over the French at the Battle of Puebla in 1862. It is celebrated regionally in Mexico and in some parts of the United States with large Mexican populations. For my family, it's an excuse to cook up some of that delicious south-of-the-border food!

Paula's Pearls of Wisdom
Use only quality tequila for the best margaritas.

MENU

Sangria

Margaritas

Green Chili Squares

Macho Nachos

Guacamole and Homemade Salsa
with Chips

Enchiladas de Pollo (Cream
Cheese and Chicken Enchiladas)

Arroz con Tomate (Red Rice)

Margarita Mousse

SANGRIA

Sweet wine flavored with citrus is a favorite at Mexican fiestas.

1 cup sugar
1 orange, thinly sliced
1 lime, thinly sliced
1 liter dry red wine
Club soda

1. Combine the sugar and 2 cups water in a small saucepan. Bring to a boil, reduce the heat, and simmer for 5 minutes to make a simple syrup. Add the orange and lime slices to the syrup. Allow to cool to room temperature, transfer to a container, and chill, covered, overnight in the refrigerator.

2. To serve: In a large pitcher, combine the syrup, fruit, and wine. Pour the sangria into wineglasses and top off each serving with a dash of club soda.

Serves 8

MARGARITAS

If I'm going to drink, I want a good margarita!

FOR EACH DRINK

Lime wedge
Kosher salt
2 ounces tequila
½ cup cracked ice
Juice of ½ lime
2 to 3 dashes triple sec or
   Curaçao

1. Take the lime wedge and rub it around the rim of a cocktail glass. Dip the glass into salt to frost the rim.

2. In a shaker, place the tequila, cracked ice, lime juice, and triple sec. Shake all of the ingredients until the ice is almost melted. Pour with ice slivers into the glass.

GREEN CHILI SQUARES

This is a quiche without the crust. The squares look pretty on the plate next to the enchiladas loaded down with toppings.

Three 4-ounce cans diced
   green chilies, with juice
2 cups (½ pound) grated
   Monterey Jack cheese
2 cups (½ pound) grated sharp
   Cheddar cheese
½ teaspoon salt
½ teaspoon pepper
Splash of hot sauce
6 eggs, beaten

1. Preheat the oven to 300°F. Spray a 12 by 8-inch baking dish with vegetable oil cooking spray.

2. Spread out the diced green chilies evenly over the bottom of the dish. Mix the cheeses together and sprinkle them evenly over the chilies.

3. Add the salt, pepper, and hot sauce to the beaten eggs. Pour the eggs over the chilies and cheese. Pat the mixture down with the back of a spoon.

4. Bake for 45 minutes, until the center is firm. Allow to sit for about 10 minutes, then cut into small squares with a bread knife. Serve warm.

Makes about 24 pieces

MACHO NACHOS

This is a winner every time you serve it.

One 13.5-ounce bag white
    corn tortilla chips
One 16-ounce can refried
    beans, traditional, lowfat, or
    vegetarian
1 medium yellow onion,
    chopped
1 cup (¼ pound) shredded
    pepper Jack cheese
1 fresh or pickled jalapeño
    pepper, seeds and veins
    removed, very finely sliced
    crosswise, plus extra for
    garnish
One 15-ounce can chili, with
    or without beans
1 cup (¼ pound) grated sharp
    Cheddar cheese
1 cup sour cream
½ cup chopped green onions
1 tomato, diced

1. Preheat the oven to 350°F.

2. On a large ovenproof platter, spread out a layer of tortilla chips. In a small saucepan over low heat, warm the refried beans until they are loose enough to spoon onto the chips. Put a teaspoon of beans on each chip. Working quickly, sprinkle the chips with onion, Jack cheese, and jalapeño slices. Spoon on the chili and top with the Cheddar.

3. Place the platter in the oven and bake until the cheeses have melted, 5 to 10 minutes.

4. Remove from the oven and place on a trivet or heatproof surface. Top the nachos with the sour cream, green onions, diced tomato, and extra jalapeño slices, for garnish. Serve hot.

Serves 10

GUACAMOLE

Guacamole is easy to make if you have a good, ripe (soft to the touch) avocado. Guacamole is also easy to buy, if you're short on time!

2 ripe avocados
1 tablespoon fresh lemon juice
1 tablespoon grated yellow
    onion
¼ teaspoon salt
½ teaspoon chili powder
⅓ cup sour cream
¼ cup diced tomato (optional)

In a glass dish, mash the avocados with the back of a fork. Add the lemon juice, onion, salt, chili powder, and sour cream. Mix well. Gently stir in the tomato, if desired. Cover with plastic wrap and store in the refrigerator until ready to use.

Serves 10 to 12

HOMEMADE SALSA

3 large ripe tomatoes, diced,
    or one 14.5-ounce can
    diced tomatoes, with juice
1 small yellow onion, finely
    chopped
1 small green bell pepper,
    finely chopped
1 small fresh jalapeño pepper,
    seeds and veins removed,
    and minced
One 4-ounce can chopped
    green chilies, with juice
1 clove garlic, minced
2 tablespoons red wine
    vinegar
1 tablespoon olive oil

Combine all of the ingredients in a medium glass bowl. Stir well with a spoon. Cover with plastic wrap and chill until serving time. Serve with corn chips.

Serves 6 to 8

ENCHILADAS DE POLLO (CREAM CHEESE AND CHICKEN ENCHILADAS)

Don't make these up too far ahead of the party, as they can get soggy. Go ahead and make the filling, and then assemble the enchiladas an hour or so before you want to cook them. Allow one enchilada per person; for a large crowd, you can even cut the enchiladas in half.

4 large chicken breasts, roasted or boiled, skin and bones removed, meat shredded

One 8-ounce package cream cheese, at room temperature

One 10.75-ounce can condensed cream of chicken soup

Two 4-ounce cans diced green chilies, with juice

6 green onions, chopped, including green tops

20 to 24 flour tortillas (7-inch diameter)

Two 10-ounce cans enchilada sauce

2 cups (½ pound) grated Monterey Jack cheese

4 cups (1 pound) grated sharp Cheddar cheese

Sour cream, for garnish

Shredded lettuce, for garnish

Diced tomatoes, for garnish

Salsa, store-bought or homemade, for garnish

1. Preheat the oven to 250°F. Spray two 13 by 9-inch casserole dishes with vegetable oil cooking spray.

2. Combine the chicken, cream cheese, soup, chilies, and green onions. Spoon 2 tablespoons of this mixture onto each tortilla and roll up.

3. Pour a very small amount of the enchilada sauce on the bottom of each casserole dish and tilt the dish so that the sauce covers the bottom. Place the enchiladas side by side on top of the sauce. When all of the enchiladas have been rolled and placed in the dishes, take the remaining enchilada sauce and pour it over the top of the enchiladas. Combine the Monterey Jack and Cheddar cheeses and sprinkle evenly over the casseroles.

4. Cover the dishes with foil and bake for 30 minutes. Uncover and bake for 10 more minutes. To serve, cut between the enchiladas and serve from the dish. Have bowls of sour cream, shredded lettuce, diced tomatoes, and salsa, for garnish.

Makes 20 to 24 enchiladas

ARROZ CON TOMATE (RED RICE)

In Savannah, red rice is often served in place of potatoes. Here's the Low-Country version of the Mexican staple.

8 slices bacon

1 medium yellow onion, chopped

2 celery stalks, chopped

1 small green bell pepper, chopped

2 cups white rice

One 14.5-ounce can stewed tomatoes

1 cup regular or spicy tomato juice

1 teaspoon sugar

1 teaspoon salt

¼ teaspoon black pepper

¼ teaspoon cayenne pepper

2 drops hot sauce

1. Preheat the oven to 325°F. Spray a 3-quart baking dish with vegetable oil cooking spray.

2. Fry the bacon until it is crisp in a heavy Dutch oven. Remove the bacon and drain it on paper towels. Sauté the onion, celery, and green pepper over low heat in the bacon grease until the vegetables are soft, about 5 minutes. Crumble the bacon and return it to the pot. Add the rice and stir well to coat it with the drippings.

3. Whirl the tomatoes in the blender briefly until they are chopped; do not puree. In a quart measuring cup, place the tomatoes and the tomato juice. Add enough water to make 4 cups liquid. Add this to the rice mixture and stir well. Add the sugar, salt, black pepper, cayenne pepper, and hot sauce.

4. Transfer the rice to the prepared baking dish. Bake for 45 minutes, covered, until the rice is tender. The rice will not be sticky; it will still have a little crunch to it.

Serves 10 to 12

MARGARITA MOUSSE

Michael really doesn't like for me to cook with liqueurs. If you prefer, you can substitute tequila for the limeade and triple sec for the orange juice. This tastes like an old-fashioned lime fluff.

¾ cup sugar

1 envelope unflavored gelatin

¼ teaspoon salt

¼ cup fresh lemon juice

¼ cup fresh lime juice

¼ cup frozen limeade concentrate (thawed) or tequila

¼ cup fresh orange juice or triple sec

4 eggs, separated

1 teaspoon grated lime zest

⅔ teaspoon cream of tartar

1 cup whipping cream, whipped until stiff

Lime slices, for garnish

1. In a medium saucepan, combine ¼ cup of the sugar, the gelatin, and the salt. Stir in the lemon juice, lime juice, limeade, and orange juice. Stir well. In a medium glass dish, whip the egg yolks until they are light. Stir them into the saucepan and cook over low heat, stirring constantly, until the gelatin is dissolved, about 3 minutes. Remove from the heat.

2. Stir in the lime zest. Transfer to a plastic container and allow to come to room temperature. Cover and refrigerate, stirring occasionally, until the mixture has begun to gel, about 30 minutes.

3. In a large bowl, beat the egg whites and cream of tartar until foamy. Add the remaining ½ cup sugar gradually, beating constantly, until the sugar has dissolved and the egg whites are stiff and glossy. Thoroughly fold together the gelled mixture, the egg whites, and the whipped cream.

4. Place in a glass soufflé dish and chill until firm. Garnish with lime slices.

Serves 10 to 12

THE AMERICAN EGG BOARD STATES:

There have been warnings against consuming raw or lightly cooked eggs on the grounds that the egg may be contaminated with salmonella, a bacteria responsible for a type of food-borne illness. Raw eggs should not be eaten by the very young, the very old, pregnant women, or anyone with a compromised immune system. Healthy people need to remember that there is a very small risk and treat eggs and other raw animal foods accordingly. Use only properly refrigerated, clean, sound-shelled, fresh, grade AA or A eggs. Avoid mixing yolks and whites with the shell.

❖ BRANDON'S DECORATING TIPS ❖

This should be a casual, colorful, fun party! Hang piñatas from the chandeliers. Use Mexican blankets as tablecloths. Tie a sombrero on the back of each chair, and look for colorful napkin rings. Hollow out red, green, and yellow bell peppers and use them as small vases for orange and yellow flowers.

Mother's Day Tea

*W*hen I was twenty-three years old, my mother passed away, leaving an incredible void in my life. But I was so blessed that there were other women to nurture and love me as my mother would—my Grandmother Paul, my Grandmother Hiers, my Aunt Peggy, my Aunt Trina, my Aunt Jesse—you know these women have been there for me all of my life.

A woman doesn't have to give birth to you for you to celebrate her on Mother's Day. A perfect example is my niece, Corrie Hiers. The day that her mother, Jill, put her

Niece Corrie Hiers, me, and my beloved Aunt Peggy on one of the happiest days of my life.

in my arms, I was hopelessly and totally lost in my love for her, and I know the feeling has been mutual over the twenty-five-year span of her life.

So if you're like me and have many women in your life whom you would like to make feel special, here's a great idea for an old-fashioned tea. You'll want to plan to have this the Saturday before Mother's Day so that you'll be able to be with your own family that Sunday. You may want to invite some little girls, too, because very few of them have probably ever been to a real tea.

This is an occasion to get out your silver tea service if you have one, or your prettiest china teapot if you don't. Give each guest of honor a personalized Mother's Day card that explains why she was invited. Oh, and be sure to have plenty of tissues handy!

Afternoon tea is an English tradition, and since Savannah was founded by the English, it is the perfect choice for our gathering. Tea is usually an elegant meal served between 2 and 5 P.M., and often includes small sandwiches, cakes, and cookies. There are wonderful teas available now in the grocery store, and tea bags are perfectly acceptable.

For the recipes, we turned to a facsimile edition of a handwritten Victorian recipe book, published by The Downtown Garden Club of Savannah in 1981. You'll see from these recipes that our forefathers loved to eat nuts, even with cheese, and our foremothers loved to use 'em!

Paula's Pearls of Wisdom

Bless the woman who has a mother's heart.

MENU

Petticoat Tails
Pecan Squares
Lemon Cups
Cheese Sandwiches
Cucumber Sandwiches
Ham Salad Sandwiches
Ginger-Nut Sandwiches
Assorted Teas*
Sugar Cubes, Lemon and Orange
Slices, Milk, Mint*

*No recipe

PETTICOAT TAILS

This shortbread cookie is made with only three ingredients. How simple is that!

2½ cups all-purpose flour
½ cup confectioners' sugar
1 cup (2 sticks) butter, cut into
   chunks, at room
   temperature

1. Combine all of the ingredients in a food processor and process until the mixture just holds together. Dump the dough onto a lightly floured board and knead about ten turns, until it is smooth. Roll into a log and wrap in waxed paper. Place in the refrigerator for 2 hours.

2. Preheat the oven to 325°F.

3. Slice the roll thin, about ¼ inch thick, and place slices on an ungreased cookie sheet. Bake for 15 minutes, until very lightly browned.

4. Cool on wire racks. Store in airtight tins.

Makes about 36 cookies, depending on the diameter of the roll

PECAN SQUARES

This is an old-fashioned boiled cookie. I cut these into very tiny pieces, as they are very sweet, like a praline.

4 eggs
One 1-pound box light brown
    sugar
1½ cups all-purpose flour
½ teaspoon baking powder
1 teaspoon vanilla extract
1½ cups chopped pecans

1. Preheat the oven to 350°F. Spray a 13 by 9-inch pan with vegetable oil cooking spray and dust with flour.

2. In a medium bowl, beat the eggs with a whisk. Stir in the brown sugar until smooth. Pour into the top of a double boiler. Cook the mixture over simmering water for 20 minutes, stirring constantly, until it reaches the soft boil stage on a candy thermometer, 240°F. Let cool for 5 minutes.

3. Sift the flour and baking powder together. Stir into the cooked mixture. Add the vanilla and pecans and stir until combined. (The batter will be thin.) Pour the batter into the prepared pan and place the pan in the oven. Bake for 12 minutes.

4. Allow to cool completely in the pan before cutting into pieces. Store in the refrigerator in an airtight tin.

Makes 48 pieces

LEMON CUPS

Crisp phyllo cups are filled with tangy lemon curd. They're so good with tea! Don't fill the cups until the last minute or they'll become soggy.

3 large lemons
1 cup sugar
4 eggs
½ cup (1 stick) butter
Two 15-count packages frozen
    mini phyllo (filo) shells,
    thawed
Slivers of fresh fruit—
    strawberries or kiwi—or
    blueberries, for garnish
    (optional)

1. Grate the zest from the lemons, then juice the lemons. Combine the zest and sugar in the bowl of a food processor fitted with the steel blade and process to mix. Add the lemon juice and eggs and process until blended.

2. Melt the butter in a double boiler. Add the egg mixture to the butter and stir until blended. Cook over medium-low heat until the mixture thickens, about 5 minutes.

3. Pour the lemon curd into a plastic container with a lid and allow to cool. Refrigerate until ready to use.

4. Spoon or pipe the cold lemon filling into the phyllo shells. Garnish with fresh fruit, if desired. Serve at once.

Makes 24 to 30 cups

{ Notes: Phyllo cups may be stored frozen, refrigerated, or at room temperature. If frozen, thaw at room temperature for 10 minutes. The cups may also be heated for extra crispness. Place the shells on a baking sheet and bake for 3 minutes at 350°F. Allow the shells to cool before filling. }

CHEESE SANDWICHES

Cheese, pecans, and pepper? It's delicious, I promise!

2 cups (½ pound) grated
   Cheddar cheese
½ cup finely chopped pecans
½ cup mayonnaise, plus extra
   for spreading on the bread
1 tablespoon grated yellow
   onion
¼ teaspoon black pepper
⅛ teaspoon cayenne pepper
One 1-pound loaf thin-sliced
   white bread (store brand or
   Pepperidge Farm)

In a medium bowl, combine the cheese, pecans, mayonnaise, onion, black pepper, and cayenne pepper. Mix well. Spread some mayonnaise on one side of each slice of the bread, then spread with the cheese mixture and top with a second slice. Trim the crusts, if desired, and cut into triangles or fingers.

Makes 12 to 15 sandwiches, enough for 24 to 30 triangles or 36 to 45 fingers

CUCUMBER SANDWICHES

I like to use thin-skinned English cucumbers (also called hothouse cucumbers) for these because they have fewer seeds and a sweeter flavor than the regular supermarket variety. Mix white and pumpernickel breads for interest, if you wish.

1 English cucumber, at least
   8 inches long
1 cup mayonnaise
6 tablespoons sour cream
1 tablespoon grated yellow
   onion
½ teaspoon seasoned salt
Two 1-pound loaves thin-sliced
   bread, white or
   pumpernickel or 1 of each

1. Wash the cucumber. Take a fork and score the peel from top to bottom. Trim the ends and slice the cucumber ¼ inch thick; you should have about 25 slices. Place the slices on paper towels to drain.

2. In a small bowl, combine the mayonnaise, sour cream, onion, and seasoned salt. Using a small biscuit cutter or juice glass, cut the bread into rounds the size of the cucumber slices. Spread a bread round with the mayonnaise mixture and place a cucumber on top. Top with a second bread round.

Makes about 25 sandwiches

HAM SALAD SANDWICHES

Use the ham salad recipe on page 83. Spread both sides of the bread with butter, mayonnaise, or mustard, your choice. Spread with ham salad. Serve sandwiches whole, or trim the crusts and cut into triangles or fingers.

GINGER-NUT SANDWICHES

This was one of the most unusual sandwich spreads we found in the Garden Club book and one of the best!

1 cup chopped pecans

One 8-ounce package cream
   cheese, softened

1 cup golden raisins, left whole

2 tablespoons diced
   crystallized ginger

Orange juice to moisten, about
   1 teaspoon

One 1-pound loaf thin-sliced
   white bread (store brand or
   Pepperidge Farm)

1. Combine the pecans, cream cheese, raisins, and crystallized ginger in a small bowl, adding just enough orange juice to make the mixture a spreadable consistency. Cover and refrigerate until ready to use.

2. Spread the cheese mixture on a slice of bread and top with another slice. The filling can be made ahead, but the sandwiches are best made no more than 30 minutes before serving. Trim the crusts, if desired, and cut into triangles or fingers.

Makes 12 to 15 sandwiches, enough for 24 to 30 triangles or 36 to 45 fingers

Graduation Potato Bar

*I*n Albany, Georgia, where I was raised, high school graduations were such a big, big deal. Friends and relatives would throw parties for the graduates, their friends, and family, and we would go to one party after another. One of my favorite parties ever was the one my Aunt Peggy threw for me. It was a Coca-Cola party! Aunt Peggy and Uncle George had a beautiful yard with a birdbath in the garden; Aunt Peggy filled the birdbath with ice and had 6-inch bottles of Coke standing up in the ice. My friends and I stood around and talked and gossiped and laughed.

Go team!

When it was time to celebrate special events with my own children, they liked a baked potato bar. There's nothing any better than a steaming baked potato with a yummy topping! I put out big bowls of crisp-skinned baked potatoes with the traditional accompaniments of butter, sour cream, grated Cheddar, and crumbled bacon, and some untraditional toppings that turn the spuds into a satisfying meal.

Paula's Pearls of Wisdom

Graduations are a time to celebrate.
You have proven that you have staying power.

BAKED POTATOES WITH TRADITIONAL TOPPINGS

No matter how delicious your toppings are, some guests are going to want a plain baked potato with the usual condiments.

1 large Idaho potato per person, plus a few extras to cut in half for each teenage boy
Vegetable oil
Kosher salt
Butter
Sour cream
Grated Cheddar cheese
Bacon, fried crisp, drained, and crumbled

1. Preheat the oven to 400°F.

2. Scrub the potatoes and pat dry. Rub the skin with a paper towel soaked with vegetable oil. Sprinkle with salt. Pierce the skin of the potato in several places with the tines of a fork. Place on a cookie sheet and bake for 1 hour and 15 minutes, until the sides are soft when pressed.

3. Place in a chafing dish and serve with bowls of butter, sour cream, grated Cheddar cheese, and crumbled fried bacon, along with the chicken à la king, steak and mushroom, and creamed seafood toppings.

CHICKEN À LA KING TOPPING

This comforting dish is also delicious over rice or toast, and is a great dish to take to a new neighbor or a friend who has just come home from the hospital.

One 3- to 3½-pound chicken
1½ teaspoons salt
4 tablespoons (½ stick) butter
¼ cup all-purpose flour
2 cups whole milk
1 cup sliced fresh mushrooms
1 cup chopped green bell
    pepper
1 tablespoon chopped
    pimiento
1 tablespoon chopped
    almonds
½ cup whipping cream
¼ teaspoon pepper

1. Place the chicken in a large pot with 1 teaspoon of the salt and water to cover. Cook over medium heat until the chicken is tender, about 1 hour. Remove the skin and bones and cut the meat into 1-inch pieces. Reserve 1 cup of the broth.

2. Make a white sauce by melting the butter in a heavy medium saucepan over low heat. Stir in the flour and whisk until it becomes a paste. Slowly add the milk, stirring constantly with a wooden spoon; you don't want any lumps! Cook until thick, about 4 minutes.

3. Add the chicken, mushrooms, green pepper, pimiento, and almonds. Add the cream, the remaining ½ teaspoon salt, and the pepper. Cook for about 5 minutes. Add about ½ cup chicken broth if the mixture is too thick. Keep hot in a chafing dish over very low heat.

4. Serve over baked potatoes.

Serves 8

STEAK AND MUSHROOM TOPPING

This is for people like me—meat and potato eaters.

1 tablespoon vegetable oil

2 pounds top round steak, sliced into thin strips

1 large yellow onion, cut into thin slices

2 tablespoons (¼ stick) butter

2 tablespoons all-purpose flour

One 10.75-ounce can condensed beef broth

8 ounces fresh mushrooms, sliced

1 teaspoon Worcestershire sauce

Salt and pepper

1 cup sour cream

1. In a large frying pan over medium-high heat, heat the oil and brown the steak strips and onion.

2. Remove the steak and onion from the pan. Add the butter and melt over low heat. Whisk in the flour and stir with a wooden spoon until smooth. Whisk in the beef broth and cook until the mixture thickens slightly, about 2 minutes.

3. Return the beef and onion to the pan. Add the mushrooms. Simmer for 30 minutes, until tender. Taste, then season with the Worcestershire sauce and salt and pepper. The topping can be refrigerated, covered, at this point.

4. Just before serving, reheat gently, and stir in the sour cream. Do not allow the topping to boil. Keep hot in a chafing dish over very low heat.

5. Serve over baked potatoes.

Serves 8

CREAMED SEAFOOD TOPPING

This is for seafood lovers.

6 tablespoons (¾ stick) butter
1 small yellow onion, chopped
1 green bell pepper, chopped
3 tablespoons all-purpose flour
1½ cups half-and-half
2 slices toast made from white
   or wheat bread, crumbled
   into small pieces
1 teaspoon ketchup
½ teaspoon prepared mustard,
   Dijon or deli
2 teaspoons fresh lemon juice
1 pound fresh crabmeat,
   picked through twice for
   shells, or 2 cups cooked,
   chopped shrimp
Salt and pepper

1. Melt 2 tablespoons of the butter in a large saucepan. Sauté the onion and green pepper until tender.

2. In a small saucepan, make a white sauce by melting the remaining 4 tablespoons butter over low heat. Whisk in the flour and slowly add the half-and-half. Stir until thick, about 2 minutes.

3. Add the sautéed vegetables, the toast, ketchup, mustard, and lemon juice. Add the crabmeat or shrimp to the sauce. Add salt and pepper to taste. Warm gently.

4. Serve over baked potatoes.

Serves 8

{ Note: If the mixture becomes too thick, add a little chicken broth to thin. Keep hot in a chafing dish over very low heat. }

SPINACH SALAD

This dressing is so good, you just might want to drink it.

One 10- to 12-ounce bag
    fresh baby spinach
4 strips bacon, fried crisp,
    drained, and crumbled
2 hard-boiled eggs, chopped
1 cup sliced fresh mushrooms
2 green onions, sliced
6 cherry tomatoes, halved

DRESSING
1 cup vegetable oil
¼ cup red wine vinegar
¼ cup fresh lemon juice
1 teaspoon salt
½ teaspoon pepper
1 tablespoon sugar
1 teaspoon dry mustard
1 clove garlic, minced

1. In a large glass bowl, layer the salad ingredients beginning with the spinach. Cover and chill.

2. Combine the dressing ingredients in a blender or in a jar with a tight-fitting lid. Shake well.

3. Add the dressing just before serving the salad and toss well.

Serves 8

SAVANNAH SHEET CAKE

This batter is very thin, but it bakes into a moist chocolate cake begging for chocolate-pecan icing.

½ cup (1 stick) butter
½ cup vegetable oil
¼ cup cocoa
2 cups all-purpose flour
2 cups sugar
½ teaspoon salt
1 teaspoon baking soda
2 eggs
½ cup sour cream
1 teaspoon vanilla extract

ICING
½ cup (1 stick) butter
¼ cup cocoa
6 tablespoons milk
One 1-pound box
   confectioners' sugar, sifted
1 teaspoon vanilla extract
1 cup finely chopped pecans,
   toasted

1. Preheat the oven to 375°F. Grease and flour a 13 by 9-inch baking pan.

2. In a small saucepan, measure 1 cup water. Add the butter, oil, and cocoa and bring the mixture to a boil. Remove from the heat.

3. Stir together the flour, sugar, salt, and baking soda in a large bowl. Beat in the eggs, sour cream, and the cocoa mixture. Add the vanilla. Mix until very smooth, about 2 minutes.

4. Pour the batter into the prepared pan. Bake for 25 to 30 minutes, until the center appears firm and the cake has begun to pull away from the sides of the pan. Let cool 12 to 15 minutes in the pan before frosting.

5. To make the icing: Boil the butter, cocoa, and milk in a medium saucepan. Remove from the heat. Stir in the sugar and beat with an electric mixer for 2 minutes. Stir in the vanilla and pecans. Pour the warm icing over the warm cake. Spread evenly.

6. Let cool about 2 hours before cutting. Refrigerate leftovers, if necessary, in a plastic container with a snap-on lid.

Makes 28 pieces

CHOCOLATE CHIP–COFFEE COOKIES

These are just downright delicious, ya'll. You'll need to make two batches—one to get eaten up while you're cooking and another to save for the party. Put them in resealable plastic freezer bags and freeze them. Take them out that morning and they'll taste like you just baked them.

½ cup (1 stick) butter, softened
1 cup light brown sugar
¼ cup granulated sugar
1 egg
2 teaspoons vanilla extract
1¾ cups all-purpose flour
½ teaspoon baking soda
½ teaspoon baking powder
½ teaspoon salt
1½ teaspoons instant coffee, powdered or freeze-dried
One 6-ounce bag chocolate chips (1 cup)
½ cup chopped pecans, lightly toasted

1. Preheat the oven to 375°F. Line a cookie sheet with parchment paper.

2. In a large mixing bowl, using an electric mixer, cream the butter and sugars until light and fluffy. Beat in the egg and vanilla. Sift together the flour, baking soda, baking powder, and salt. Add the dry ingredients to the butter mixture and, using a spatula, stir together until they are completely blended. Stir in the instant coffee, chocolate chips, and pecans.

3. Drop by tablespoonfuls, 1 inch apart, onto the prepared cookie sheet. Bake in batches for 11 minutes, until crisp on the bottom. (Reuse parchment paper for each batch.)

4. Remove the cookie sheet from the oven and allow the cookies to cool undisturbed for about 3 minutes, then transfer to a wire cooling rack to cool completely before storing in airtight tins or freezer bags.

Makes about 24 cookies

Roll up your napkins and use tassels as napkin rings. Roll up the invitations to look like diplomas and mail them in tubes. Magnolias are always blooming here at graduation, and it would be lovely just to go cut them and place them throughout the house. The smell is intoxicating. If you can't get magnolias, any fragrant spring flower, such as peonies and lilacs, would be lovely.

Father's Day Boating Picnic

If I could choose the perfect day for a boating picnic, it would be Father's Day. A boating picnic is one of my favorite things to do—nothing stimulates your appetite like the water, and there ain't nothing no better than food on a boat. My Granddaddy and Grandmama Paul were big fishermen. I remember going down to Florida and visiting them. When we went out on the boat, Grandmama would pack a lunch—a can of sardines, saltine crackers, a sliced onion, and mustard! That food tasted so stinking good out on that water! My granddaddy would go onto the sandbars and scoop out the oysters and crack them open and eat them as soon as he pulled them out of the water.

Michael has lived his whole life in one place—the spot where we built our house. He loves the water so much he had to figure out how to make a living on it, so he

Me and my daddy.

133

became a harbor pilot, the guy who gets on ships in the ocean channel and navigates them to the docks. When I'm planning our Father's Day celebration, it's only natural that we would wind up on a boat with picnic baskets filled with delicious food!

Paula's Pearls of Wisdom

The greatest gift in the world is to be the child of a loving father.

BAKED OLIVE PUFFS

This recipe has been around forever, but these are just the right size for a picnic, and I just love the taste of olives and sharp Cheddar.

1 cup (¼ pound) grated sharp
   Cheddar cheese
4 tablespoons (½ stick) butter,
   softened
½ cup all-purpose flour
½ teaspoon salt
½ teaspoon paprika
30 medium pimiento-stuffed
   green olives, drained

1. Line a baking sheet with parchment paper.

2. In a medium mixing bowl, combine the cheese, butter, flour, salt, and paprika. Mix with an electric mixer until blended. The dough will be quite crumbly but will come together due to the heat from your hands.

3. Pinch off a small amount of the dough, flatten it in your palm, and wrap it around an olive. Roll the olive in your hands to smooth it out. Place each olive on the baking sheet.

4. When all the olives are wrapped, cover with plastic wrap and freeze for at least 1 hour or up to 24 hours.

5. When you're ready to bake the puffs, preheat

the oven to 375°F. Take the pan with the puffs straight from the freezer, remove the plastic wrap, and bake for 18 to 20 minutes, until browned on the bottom.

Makes 30 puffs

SMOKED OYSTER LOG

My goodness, this is tasty! Spread it on your favorite cracker.

1½ packages (8 ounces each) cream cheese, softened
1 tablespoon steak sauce
2 tablespoons mayonnaise
1 clove garlic, crushed
½ small yellow onion, finely minced
One 3.75-ounce can smoked oysters, finely chopped
1½ tablespoons chili powder
1½ cups pecans, toasted and finely chopped
¼ cup minced fresh parsley
Wheat crackers (or other favorite crackers), for serving

1. Combine the cream cheese, steak sauce, mayonnaise, garlic, and onion. Blend until smooth and creamy. Stir in the smoked oysters. Form into a log about 9 inches long and wrap well in plastic wrap. Refrigerate until firm.

2. Combine the chili powder and pecans. Roll the cream cheese log in the nuts until completely coated. Then roll the log in the parsley.

3. Keep the log in a plastic bag in the cooler until you are ready to eat. Serve with crackers.

Makes one 9-inch log

GRILLED CHICKEN PITA

Don't let the long list of ingredients keep you from trying this delicious sandwich.

3 boneless, skinless chicken
breasts (about 1½ pounds)

3 tablespoons plus 2
teaspoons fresh lemon juice

3 tablespoons soy sauce

1 clove garlic, minced

2 teaspoons dried oregano

2 small tomatoes, finely
chopped

1 cup (¼ pound) crumbled
feta cheese

¼ cup olive oil

1 large Vidalia or purple
onion, cut into thin rings

6 pita breads

½ head romaine lettuce,
finely chopped

One 10.6-ounce jar kalamata
olives, drained, halved, and
pitted, or other black olives

12 slices bacon, fried crisp

Alfalfa sprouts

Salt and pepper

YOGURT SAUCE

8 ounces (1 cup) unflavored
yogurt

1 clove garlic, minced

¼ cup finely chopped walnuts

1 tablespoon olive oil

1. Rinse the chicken breasts and pat dry. Combine 3 tablespoons of the lemon juice, the soy sauce, garlic, and 1 teaspoon of the oregano in a glass dish. Add the chicken, turn to coat, and cover with plastic wrap. Allow the chicken breasts to marinate for 30 minutes at room temperature or overnight in the refrigerator.

2. Combine the tomatoes and feta cheese in a small glass dish. Add the remaining 2 teaspoons lemon juice, the olive oil, and the remaining 1 teaspoon oregano, and stir to combine. Allow to sit at room temperature for 30 minutes.

3. Make the yogurt sauce: In a small bowl, whisk together the yogurt, garlic, walnuts, and olive oil. Cover and refrigerate until ready to use.

4. Prepare the grill. Spray a grill basket with olive oil. Grill the chicken breasts over medium heat for 8 to 10 minutes, until no longer pink in the thickest portion of each breast. Spread the onion rings over the surface of the basket and grill while the chicken is cooking. Turn the basket frequently. The onion rings will blacken as they cook; this will also take 8 to 10 minutes.

5. When the chicken and onion rings are cooked, place the pita breads on the grill for about 2 minutes per side, until grill marks show. Slice the chicken into very thin pieces.

6. At serving time, put out all of the ingredients and allow each person to assemble sandwiches: Slit each pita. Place several slices of grilled chicken, 3 or 4 slivers of grilled onion, a tablespoon of tomato-feta mixture, lettuce, olives, and 1 or 2 slices of bacon

into each pita. Top with yogurt sauce and a wad of alfalfa sprouts. Add salt and pepper to taste. Fold up the sides of the pita and enjoy!

Serves 6

{ Note: If serving sandwiches on the go, store each ingredient in a separate plastic bag or covered container and place in a cooler. }

MACARONI SALAD

I make my macaroni salad just like I do my potato salad, and mix it up and serve it warm. For a picnic, I'd store it in the refrigerator, then pack it in a cooler. Be sure to taste it before you leave; you may need a little more mayo, as the noodles really soak up the sauce.

2 cups cooked elbow macaroni (about 1½ cups uncooked), drained and cooled after cooking (not rinsed)
¼ cup chopped green onions
1 cup chopped celery
3 hard-boiled eggs, chopped
¼ cup chopped green bell pepper
¼ cup diced pimiento
1 teaspoon lemon-pepper seasoning (optional)
1 teaspoon House Seasoning (page 147)
1 tablespoon Dijon mustard
¼ cup mayonnaise
¾ cup sour cream

In a large bowl, combine the macaroni, green onions, celery, eggs, bell pepper, and pimiento. In a small bowl, stir together the lemon-pepper seasoning, House Seasoning, mustard, mayonnaise, and sour cream. Mix the dressing gently with the other ingredients. Cover and chill until serving time. Taste and add additional salt if necessary.

Serves 6

CHOCOLATE CHEWY COOKIES

These cookies are best eaten within twenty-four hours, which is usually not a problem.

2 cups confectioners' sugar,
    sifted
2 tablespoons cocoa, sifted
¼ teaspoon salt
⅓ cup all-purpose flour, sifted
3 egg whites
1 cup chopped pecans,
    toasted

1. Preheat the oven to 350°F. Line two baking sheets with parchment paper.

2. Stir together the sugar, cocoa, salt, and flour. Add the egg whites one at a time. Beat well, then stir in the pecans. The batter will be very thin.

3. Drop by tablespoonfuls onto the prepared baking sheets. Bake for 12 to 15 minutes, until the cookies have begun to brown on the bottom and appear "set." Allow to sit for about 2 minutes undisturbed, then remove the cookies to wire racks to cool completely. Store in airtight containers.

Makes 18 big cookies

❖ BRANDON'S DECORATING TIPS ❖

A box lunch would be the way to go for this party, but the boxes would be very manly. Pay a visit to a cigar shop in your area; they usually have cigar boxes in the back that they will give away. Line each box with a brightly colored napkin, pack it with lunch, and tie with a matching ribbon.

ALL TOGETHER

What comes to my mind when you say the word "celebration" is any time when we're all together. It doesn't have to be a birthday or Christmas. Because of our restaurants (The Lady & Sons and Uncle Bubba's Oyster House) being so time-consuming, a celebration for me is just a Sunday afternoon at Paula's house when all of the family is together. It's the end of a successful week, we're all together, and we're thankful for what we have—for the many blessings and responsibilities that have been put on us. This past Christmas Eve, I had both my kids, Corrie and Jay, in town, and Paula and Mike came to my house, and we just had chickens on the grill. We sat around and talked and laughed and talked and laughed. That's a celebration.

Food has always been a big part of our celebrations. I seem to like every-thing—outdoor grilling, country cooking, and seafood. Luckily, I'm not allergic

With my brother, Bubba. See the resemblance?

to anything! We live in this beautiful coastal city, and to me, one of the best dishes around is just a good old Low-Country boil—sausage, fresh Georgia shrimp, potatoes, corn, blue crab that you've caught yourself. Boil it, dump it out on newspaper, and then it's grab and growl time. And speaking of growling, our family get-togethers wouldn't be the same without all the family dogs. We're all big dog lovers, and by the time you get them all together, we have five of 'em and they get so excited all being together. They love swimming in the creek and running around and chasing balls and hoping for a piece of sausage! Celebrations just wouldn't be the same without 'em.

Earl "Bubba" Hiers

Fourth of July Outdoor Grill Party
and Low-Country Boil

The Fourth of July just has to be spent outdoors. I am lucky enough to live in a perfect spot for outdoor celebrating—my house sits right on a creek, and we might see several shrimp boats a day go by. I just love it when all of my family gathers, and the dogs are running around, and everyone—including the dogs—cools off in the creek. When we built our new house, we made a covered outdoor kitchen that we call Michael's smokehouse. We put in an ice maker, a sink, a refrigerator—everything we need to make outdoor cooking convenient. It sits twenty feet from the water, so Michael can tend the brisket while he's enjoying the festivities!

The Lady & Sons.

I've included our recipe for Low-Country boil because that's probably the number one favorite at our house for summer entertaining. You can put all kinds of things in a Low-Country boil, but I really like mine with just sausage, new potatoes, corn if you can get it fresh, and, finally, big old wild Georgia shrimp. Our Low-County boils are so good because we don't skimp on the quality of the shrimp—we use those big, juicy 16 to 20 count shrimp—and we take care not to overcook 'em. I don't eat many because I just love the sausage, but there's always somebody else to eat my share! We might throw in some crab legs or blue crab if Bobby's caught some off his dock. We season our pot with Old Bay. And if we have potatoes, my family insists on my serving my potato sauce. You just throw it all out on the table and everybody gets to diggin' in! Then, after everybody's cooled off in the creek, serve a flag cake or go inside and sit down with a big old slice of mud pie. So, hang the flag and let's get to celebrating!

Paula's Pearls of Wisdom

I was fortunate enough to be born in the land of the free, but my own personal freedom came about by taking responsibility for myself.

CRABBIES

These are soooooo good!

½ cup (1 stick) butter, softened

8 ounces (1 cup) sharp
  Cheddar cheese spread,
  any variety

2 teaspoons mayonnaise

¼ teaspoon garlic powder

½ teaspoon seasoned salt

½ pound fresh crabmeat,
  picked through twice for
  shells

6 regular-size English muffins,
  split

Paprika

1. In a medium bowl, combine the butter, cheese spread, mayonnaise, garlic powder, and seasoned salt. Mix well. Gently fold in the crabmeat.

2. Spread the mixture on the muffin halves and sprinkle with paprika. Cut into quarters. Place on a baking sheet and cover with plastic wrap. Freeze for 20 minutes.

3. While the crabbies are freezing, preheat the oven to 350°F.

4. Remove the plastic wrap and bake the frozen crabbies for 20 minutes, until the topping is browned and bubbly.

Makes 48 crabbies

TEXAS BRISKET

When I fixed this brisket on my show, I cooked it for five hours, and lots of viewers wrote in to say they made it, and how moist and delicious it was. Later on, when I visited the Memphis barbecue festival, I learned that the real brisket cookers smoke their meat for ten to twelve hours! We tested this on a conventional charcoal grill and a gas grill. The flavor using charcoal was better, but you can't beat the ease of a gas grill; it's so easy to control the temperature. The most important thing is to allow enough time to cook the meat until it's falling-apart tender.

One 5- to 6-pound brisket, trimmed, but left with a layer of fat about ¼ inch thick
6 tablespoons House Seasoning (below)
3 tablespoons chili powder
1½ teaspoons dark brown sugar
1½ teaspoons onion powder
1 teaspoon dried oregano
1 teaspoon cayenne pepper
6 cups hickory wood chips, soaked in water for 30 minutes

1. Rinse the brisket thoroughly under cold water and pat dry with paper towels. In a small bowl, mix together the House Seasoning, chili powder, sugar, onion powder, oregano, and cayenne. Rub the brisket with the spice rub on all sides. Place the brisket fat side up in a large disposable aluminum pan and let it sit while your grill/smoker heats.

2. Follow the directions on your grill/smoker for indirect grilling. Place the soaked chips into the chip box, or make a pouch with tinfoil for the chips and place the pouch directly on the coals. Place the pan with the brisket in the center of the grate and cover the grill.

3. Slow-grill the brisket until it is tender and an instant-read thermometer inserted in the center of the meat reads about 190°F, 10 to 12 hours. Add coals and wood chips as necessary to maintain a low temperature, 250°F to 300°F.

4. Transfer the brisket to a cutting board to rest for about 30 minutes. (The meat will shred if you try to slice it right off the grill.) Slice the brisket across the grain to serve.

Serves 10 to 12

HOUSE SEASONING

You will notice I call for this in many recipes. I can't cook without it!

1 cup table salt
¼ cup pepper
¼ cup garlic powder

Mix the ingredients together and store in an airtight container for up to 6 months. Use as a seasoning on meat and when cooking vegetables.

Makes 1½ cups

SLOW COOKER PINTO BEANS

1 pound dried pinto beans
1 teaspoon chili powder
½ teaspoon dried oregano
½ pound ham hocks, or
 ¼ pound streak o' lean
1 yellow onion, chopped
2 tablespoons (¼ stick) butter
 (optional)
1 tablespoon House Seasoning
 (above)

1. Wash the beans and soak overnight in cold water. Or use the quick method and boil the beans in plenty of water for 2 minutes, then allow to sit for 1 hour.

2. Drain the beans and dump them into the slow cooker. Stir in the chili powder and oregano.

3. If using ham hocks, soak in a separate pot in 4 cups water for 2 hours. Add the ham hocks and soaking liquid to the slow cooker. If using streak o' lean, cut the meat into chunks and brown in a skillet. Remove the meat and put it in the slow cooker with the beans.

4. Sauté the onion in the fat in the skillet or sauté the onion in 2 tablespoons butter. Add the onion to the beans. Add the House Seasoning. Stir well.

5. Cover and cook on high until the beans are tender and have absorbed most of the liquid, about 5 hours.

Serves 10 to 12

HOT SLAW

This colorful side is a great alternative to a salad or traditional coleslaw made with mayonnaise. It makes a large quantity, and if you have leftovers, use it as a topping for a barbecue or grilled chicken breast sandwich. Delicious!

6 slices bacon

1 large yellow onion, chopped

1 medium green bell pepper, chopped

1 medium (3 pounds) head green cabbage, quartered, cored, and shredded

¼ cup chili powder

Kosher salt

One 14.5-ounce can diced tomatoes and green chilies

1. In a 12-inch skillet, cook the bacon until crisp. Remove the bacon to paper towels to drain, but leave the grease in the skillet. Crumble the bacon and set aside.

2. In the reserved bacon grease, cook the onion and green pepper until limp, about 5 minutes. Add the cabbage and cook until limp but not soft, 3 to 5 minutes. Add the chili powder and salt to taste. Add the tomatoes and simmer until just heated through. The slaw should be slightly crisp. Adjust seasoning and sprinkle the crumbled bacon over the top.

Serves 10 to 12

Crème de Menthe Brownies (page 73)

Left: Buffalo Chicken Wings (page 184); right: Teriyaki Chicken Wings (page 184)

On the serving stand, top to bottom: Lemon Cups (page 119), Pecan Squares (page 118), Petticoat Tails (page 117); on the plate, clockwise from top: Ginger-Nut Sandwiches (page 122), Cucumber Sandwiches (page 121), Cheese Sandwiches (page 120)

Sangria (page 106); Enchiladas de Pollo *(Cream Cheese and Chicken Enchiladas) (page 111)*;
Green Chili Squares (page 108); Arroz con Tomate *(Red Rice) (page 112)*

Small plate: Turtle Pizza (page 161); large plate: Pesto and Feta Pizza (page 158)

Grilled Chicken Pita (page 137)

*Low-Country Boil (page 149) with (clockwise from top) Cocktail Sauce (page 150),
Potato Sauce (page 150), and Tartar Sauce (page 150)*

Hummingbird Cake (page 13)

LOW-COUNTRY BOIL

ℒow-Country boil is more of a technique than a recipe, and I'm about to tell ya just how to do it so that you have the best dish you could ever hope for. You have to start with quality ingredients, and you have to follow the directions exactly to have all of the ingredients come out perfectly cooked.

Sometimes, Michael will pull out the sausage, potatoes, and corn and put them into a cooler to stay warm. Then he will cook the shrimp separately in the seasoned water. This way, there is no chance the shrimp will get overcooked.

¼ pound fully cooked smoked sausage per person, cut into 1-inch pieces

¼ cup Old Bay seasoning, or more to taste

2 small new potatoes per person

1 ear fresh corn per person, shucked, silked, and broken in half

½ pound large fresh shrimp per person (16 to 20 count size), shell on

Tartar Sauce (page 150)

Cocktail Sauce (page 150)

Potato Sauce (page 150)

Fill a large pot with enough water to cover all of the ingredients. Add the sausage and Old Bay seasoning and allow to boil for about 20 minutes so that the sausage can flavor the water. Taste, and add more Old Bay if you think you need more. Add the potatoes and boil for about 15 minutes. Add the corn and boil about 10 minutes more. Finally, add the shrimp and allow to cook for 3 minutes. Taste a shrimp and if it is cooked through, drain immediately and serve on an oversize platter or, as we do, on a table covered with newspaper! Serve with the three sauces.

TARTAR SAUCE

Leftovers will keep, covered and refrigerated, about two weeks. Great with any seafood.

½ cup chopped green onion
½ cup chopped dill pickle
1½ cups mayonnaise
½ teaspoon House Seasoning
  (page 147)
1 teaspoon dried dill weed

In a glass dish, stir together all of the ingredients. Cover and refrigerate until serving time.

Makes about 2 cups

COCKTAIL SAUCE

Leftovers will keep, covered and refrigerated, about two weeks. Delicious with fried shrimp or scallops.

2 cups ketchup
1 tablespoon prepared
  horseradish
1 tablespoon fresh lemon juice
1 teaspoon Worcestershire
  sauce

In a glass dish, stir together all of the ingredients. Cover and refrigerate until serving time.

Makes about 2¼ cups

POTATO SAUCE

If I serve potatoes and no potato sauce, I am in trouble, big-time!

¾ cup mayonnaise
¼ cup sour cream
2 cups finely chopped yellow
  onion
Salt and pepper

In a glass dish, stir together the mayonnaise, sour cream, and onion. Add salt and pepper to taste. Cover and refrigerate until serving time. Serve with buttered new potatoes.

Makes about 3 cups

FLAG CAKE

The icing will hide any flaws in your layering.

One 6-ounce package cherry-
   flavored gelatin
One 1-pound loaf pound cake,
   any brand
Two 8-ounce packages cream
   cheese, softened
½ cup confectioners' sugar
2 cups whipping cream,
   whipped
1 pint fresh strawberries
1 pint fresh blueberries

1. Boil 1½ cups water. In a glass dish, stir the water into the gelatin, stirring about 2 minutes, until all of the gelatin is thoroughly dissolved. Add 2 cups cold water and stir. Refrigerate this mixture for about 15 minutes, until it has begun to thicken but is still loose enough to spread.

2. Spray a 13 by 9-inch baking pan with vegetable oil cooking spray. Cut the pound cake into thin slices and lay them evenly over the bottom of the pan. Spread the partially gelled gelatin evenly over the cake. Refrigerate for several hours, until the gelatin has set and formed a firm layer over the cake.

3. Beat together the cream cheese and sugar until very fluffy. Fold in the whipped cream. Spread this evenly over the gelatin layer. Refrigerate until ready to serve.

4. Not more than 30 minutes before serving, slice the strawberries in half. Decorate the top of the cake in a flag pattern, using the strawberries for the "bars" and the blueberries for the "stars."

Serves 20

MUD PIE

Make this up to a week before the party if you think you can keep it hidden until then!

1 gallon coffee ice cream
2 large toffee candy bars,
    frozen, or ½ a 10-ounce
    package toffee chips
1 jar chocolate ice cream
    topping
1 jar caramel ice cream
    topping
One 9-inch deep-dish piecrust,
    baked and cooled
1 cup whipping cream,
    whipped with 2 tablespoons
    confectioners' sugar
½ cup chopped toasted pecans

1. Allow the ice cream to soften for about 10 minutes, then put it in a large bowl. Finely crush the frozen candy bars in a food processor or in a plastic bag with a rolling pin. Stir the candy bar chunks or toffee chips into the softened ice cream.

2. Drizzle ribbons of chocolate and caramel toppings on the bottom of the piecrust. Pile the ice cream into the crust and smooth the top. Lay a piece of plastic wrap on top of the ice cream. Place the pie in the freezer to harden.

3. When the ice cream is firm, spread the top of the pie with the whipped cream. Decorate with more syrup ribbons and the toasted pecans. Refreeze. When frozen solid, store carefully in a large plastic freezer bag. Eat within a week.

Makes 6 large or 8 small servings

❖ BRANDON'S DECORATING TIPS ❖

Of course you're going to do everything in red, white, and blue. Hang red, white, and blue Japanese lanterns from the trees. To decorate your table, make topiaries in clay pots by attaching cherry tomatoes and rosemary with toothpicks snipped in half. They're beautiful and should last for over a week.

Movie-Watching Pizza Party in Bed

I've always enjoyed curling up in my bed or on my sofa and watching a good movie. Most of my family really, really enjoys watching movies, and a lot of us *love* watching movies. In fact, there's nothing better than a Saturday or a Sunday when you have nothing to do and so you turn that day into a movie marathon—I just watch one movie after another. Well, I just have to tell ya, I had an experience that really, really changed my views about movies.

I got a call one day from Gail Leven of Paramount Studios. Why was she calling me? Gail proceeded to tell me that she was casting a movie produced by Tom Cruise and directed by Cameron Crowe. She had been channel surfing while home recuperating from a minor illness when she came upon my show. There was one character in the movie she was having a hard time casting. When she saw me, she said, "Oh, my goodness, there is my Aunt Dora." Gail asked if I would consider playing the part of Aunt Dora in this movie called *Elizabethtown.*

Well, I can't tell you what a state of shock I was in. In fact, the first thing I said to Gail was, "Do you realize I'm not an actress?" And she just laughed and said, "Paula, you're further along than you think you are." Gail could hear the hesitation in my voice. She said, "I'll tell you what. There is not a nicer man around than Cameron Crowe. I want to have Cameron call you tomorrow and ya'll just talk about it." So Cameron called me the next day, and I fell in love with this man over the phone. I found him to be kind and generous and considerate and thoughtful, and I could tell immediately that he was passionate about his work. I agreed to play Aunt Dora, but I said, "Cameron, promise me one thing—that if I'm no good, you'll put my butt on the bus and send me home, because I don't want to do anything to let you down."

Well, I went to Hollywood, and I'm happy to say I didn't come back on the bus! I worked six weeks, part of it in Kentucky and part of it on a soundstage at Paramount Studios in Hollywood. You have no idea when you're sitting back and enjoying that movie at home or in the theater just how much work is involved, how many times those scenes are done over and over and over and over, how perfect the lighting has to be, how perfect the sound has to be, and then you have to shoot the scene with one camera to get one angle and then you have to shoot the same scene over again to get another camera angle. Now I look at a scene in a movie and think, "Oh, my goodness, what they must have done to get that scene shot." I have a new respect for movie makers and actors and the whole Hollywood scene. They make it look so glamorous, and I know from experience, it's not.

And speaking of movies, here's another story. A wonderful young couple in Mystic, Connecticut, won a kitchen makeover contest held by the Food Network, and I was asked to do the makeover. They had bought this little tiny hundred-year-old farmhouse. The young man was in construction and had done all the work to the house, but there was not enough money for the kitchen. Well, I was so thrilled when I went to Mystic and met 'em; I got so excited about being able to help them build their dream kitchen. Their kitchen was going to be out of commission for a while and I wanted to treat them to some southern cooking. Then the production crew called and said we're going to a little restaurant called Mystic Pizza, which was the setting for the movie *Mystic Pizza,* starring Julia Roberts. When I walked into the restaurant, there was memorabilia all over the place from the movie.

I said, "Well, you know, there ain't nothing southern about pizza! How am I going to pull this number off?" I had decided that I would freeze some collard greens and cooked ham hocks and send them up to Mystic Pizza. When I got ready to walk in the door, my collard greens and ham hocks would be there (I hoped!). Fortunately, they were. I went back into the kitchen, got my pizza crust set up, and started building this collard green pizza. I took a little bit of the restaurant's marinara sauce and mixed it with mayonnaise and cream cheese. I spread that on the bottom of the crust, and then I scattered the collards and shredded ham hock on the sauce, and I added sliced fresh mushrooms. I went through the containers of pizza toppings, saw that they had bacon, and said, "Bacon and collard greens; you can't get any better!" So I put a layer of bacon on top. I covered it with mozzarella cheese, and then I threw this pizza in the oven to bake.

Now, bear in mind that I had never made a collard green pizza, let alone heard of a collard green pizza, so I had no idea what to expect and didn't know if it would be good or not. All I could do was keep my fingers crossed. Well, you will not believe when I pulled out that pizza and served it; it was incredible, just incredible. In fact, I have to say, Mystic Pizza brought out all these different kinds of pizza for the crew to have for lunch, but you know which one was the best? The collard green pizza! It was out of this world!

Michael and I love to eat in our bed! And pizza is one of those foods where it never dawns on us to take it to the table. We just take it straight to bed and lay back and eat that yummy pizza. For dessert, you could serve Georgia Cookie Candy—what's better for movie watching than peanut butter and chocolate?—or a strawberry pizza, or a turtle pizza! Just try to resist the temptation of wiping your fingers on the sheets!

If you don't want to make your own pizza dough, I bet your local pizza parlor would sell you some! You may also use a ready-to-top pizza crust, like Boboli.

Paula's Pearls of Wisdom

This menu is dedicated to Cameron Crowe—one of the most talented, most considerate, and kindest men I have ever met. Thanks for being the one to take me on the ride of Elizabethtown.

BASIC PIZZA DOUGH

This is really easy to make and soooo much better than a bought pizza crust.

One ¼-ounce package active
   dry yeast, regular or
   RapidRise
2 teaspoons salt
4½ to 5 cups bread flour
3 tablespoons olive oil

1. Measure out 1¾ cups warm water (it should be pleasantly warm on your wrist). Sprinkle the yeast on top of the water and allow it to activate, about 10 minutes.

2. Put the salt and 2 cups of the flour into a food processor. Pulse five times to blend. Pour in the yeast and water and pulse five times. Add the olive oil. Add the remaining flour 1 cup at a time, pulsing and scraping the sides of the bowl until well blended. As soon as the mixture is combined, dump it out onto a well-floured board and knead for fifteen turns, until the dough is smooth and elastic.

3. Place the dough in a greased bowl and turn to coat all sides. Cover with plastic wrap or a tea towel. Allow the dough to rise in a warm place for about 45 minutes, until doubled in size, then punch it down. Divide it in half; each half will make one 12-inch pizza. You can make two pizzas, or freeze half the dough for another time. Freeze the dough in a reseal-

able freezer bag. To thaw, remove the bag from the freezer and place in the refrigerator for 24 hours. Roll the dough out while cold, then allow it to come to room temperature before adding toppings.

Makes enough dough for two 12-inch pizzas

COLLARD GREEN AND HAM HOCK PIZZA

Here it is! The recipe that won raves in Mystic, Connecticut.

½ recipe Basic Pizza Dough (above)

Cornmeal, for dusting

One 8-ounce package cream cheese

1 cup mayonnaise

¾ cup marinara sauce

½ cup cooked collard greens, drained

1 large ham hock, cooked and the meat removed from the bone

4 slices bacon, cut into large pieces and fried until limp but not quite crisp

1 cup (¼ pound) shredded mozzarella cheese

1. Preheat the oven to 450°F.

2. Roll out the pizza dough into a 12-inch circle. Place on a cornmeal-dusted pizza stone, pizza pan, or cookie sheet. Roll up the edge slightly to create a ridge around the pizza.

3. In a medium bowl, combine the cream cheese, mayonnaise, and ½ cup of the marinara sauce. Stir well. Spread over the pizza crust. Top with the collard greens, ham hock meat, and bacon. Cover with the cheese and distribute dollops of the remaining ¼ cup marinara sauce.

4. Bake for 16 to 18 minutes, until the cheese is bubbly and the crust is light brown.

Makes 8 slices

PESTO AND FETA PIZZA

This is a sophisticated pizza for those who don't care for tomato sauce.

½ recipe Basic Pizza Dough
(page 156)
Cornmeal, for dusting
½ cup basil pesto, homemade
or store-bought
6 sun-dried tomatoes, sliced in
ribbons
One 6-ounce jar marinated
artichoke hearts, drained
and chopped
½ cup (2 ounces) crumbled
feta cheese
½ cup diced fresh tomato,
about 1 small Roma or
½ a beefsteak
2 cups (½ pound) shredded
mozzarella cheese
Olive oil
1 teaspoon freshly grated
Parmesan cheese

1. Preheat the oven to 450°F.

2. Roll out the pizza dough into a 12-inch circle. Place on a cornmeal-dusted pizza stone, pizza pan, or cookie sheet. Roll up the edge slightly to create a ridge around the pizza. Spread the pesto over the crust. Evenly distribute the sun-dried tomatoes, artichoke hearts, feta cheese, and fresh tomato over the dough. Top with the mozzarella cheese. Brush the edge of the pizza with a pastry brush dipped in olive oil and sprinkle Parmesan cheese around the rim.

3. Bake for 16 to 18 minutes, until the cheese is bubbly and the crust is light brown.

Makes 8 slices

SCALLOPS AND BACON PIZZA

No one thought this would be good but me! Now, it's a favorite.

½ recipe Basic Pizza Dough
  (page 156)
Cornmeal, for dusting
1 cup marinara sauce, any
  brand
1 cup sour cream
½ pound bacon, cut into small
  pieces, fried crisp, and
  drained
1½ cups (6 ounces) shredded
  mozzarella cheese
½ cup freshly grated Parmesan
  cheese
6 large sea scallops, cut into
  quarters or eighths,
  depending on size

1. Preheat the oven to 450°F.

2. Roll out the pizza dough into a 12-inch circle. Place on a cornmeal-dusted pizza stone, pizza pan, or cookie sheet. Roll up the edge slightly to create a ridge around the pizza.

3. In a small bowl, stir together the marinara sauce and sour cream until thoroughly combined. Spread the mixture evenly over the crust. Distribute the bacon evenly over the sauce. Combine the mozzarella and Parmesan cheeses and sprinkle them evenly over the bacon. Top the cheese with the scallops, which should be distributed evenly over the surface of the pizza.

4. Bake the pizza for 16 to 18 minutes, until the cheese is bubbly and the scallops are cooked.

Makes 8 slices

STRAWBERRY PIZZA

My movie-watching party gives me an excuse to share this dessert pizza recipe. The crust tastes like shortbread and the topping like strawberry pie. What could be better?

1 cup (2 sticks) butter, at room temperature

2 cups all-purpose flour

1 cup finely chopped pecans

3 cups confectioners' sugar

1 cup whipping cream, whipped

One 8-ounce package cream cheese, at room temperature

1 cup granulated sugar

1 tablespoon cornstarch

One 3-ounce box strawberry gelatin (you may use sugar-free)

1 pint fresh strawberries, hulled and sliced

1. Preheat the oven to 250°F.

2. In a small bowl, mix the butter and flour until smooth. Stir in the pecans and combine. Pat the mixture out onto a 12-inch pizza pan or pizza stone, or shape into a circle on a large cookie sheet. Roll up the edge slightly to create a ridge around the pizza. Bake for about 40 minutes, until lightly browned and cooked through. Cool completely.

3. To make the second layer, in a medium bowl, stir together the confectioners' sugar, whipped cream, and cream cheese. Mix about 2 minutes, until thoroughly blended and light. Spread evenly over the cooled cookie crust. Refrigerate for 1 hour, until firm.

4. Measure 1 cup water into a small saucepan. Bring the water to a boil and stir in the granulated sugar and cornstarch. Cook for about 1 minute, stirring constantly. Stir in the package of strawberry gelatin. Allow the mixture to cool to room temperature, then spread this over the firm cream cheese layer. Refrigerate until the gelatin layer is firm, about 2 hours.

5. Decorate with fresh sliced strawberries. Refrigerate until serving time.

Serves 10 to 12, depending on the size of the slices

TURTLE PIZZA

It is hard to think about movies without thinking about candy! In keeping with the theme of this party, here's a "pizza" inspired by the flavors of the traditional Turtle.

Four 10-inch flour tortillas
One 12-ounce package
  caramel candies,
  unwrapped
½ cup sweetened condensed
  milk
1 cup chocolate chips
1 cup toasted pecan pieces

1. Preheat the oven to 350°F.

2. Cut each tortilla into 8 wedges. Bake the tortilla wedges for 7 to 9 minutes, until a light golden color. (If you try to cut the baked tortilla, it will break and crack.)

3. Combine the caramels and condensed milk in a microwave-safe glass dish. Microwave on high (100%) for 1 minute, stir, and microwave again for 1 minute. Stir again. When the caramels are melted, stir the mixture until it is smooth. Spread it evenly on the 32 tortilla wedges.

4. Melt the chocolate chips in a microwave-safe glass dish on high (100%) for 1 minute, stir, and microwave 10 seconds more. Stir until smooth. Spread the chocolate layer over the caramel layer. Sprinkle the pecans evenly over the chocolate. Refrigerate until serving time.

Makes 32 wedges

GEORGIA COOKIE CANDY

What better way to top off any pizza party than with peanut butter and chocolate?

1 cup (2 sticks) butter or margarine, softened

1 cup crunchy peanut butter

3 cups confectioners' sugar, sifted

1½ cups graham cracker crumbs

1½ cups semisweet chocolate chips

1. Line a 13 by 9 by 2-inch pan with foil.

2. Combine the butter, peanut butter, sugar, and graham cracker crumbs in a food processor. Process until the mixture forms a ball. Press into the foil-lined pan using your hands or a spatula.

3. Melt the chocolate chips in a double boiler over simmering water or in a microwave-safe glass dish in the microwave for 1 minute on high (100%). Stir. If the chocolate has not completely melted, microwave for 10 seconds more, then stir. Spread evenly over the cookie layer with a spatula. Chill for several hours.

4. When ready to serve, allow the candy to come to room temperature before cutting into pieces. Store in an airtight container in the refrigerator.

Makes 36 to 40 pieces

❖ BRANDON'S DECORATING TIPS ❖

Arrange dahlias, hydrangeas, or cockscomb in a vase and stick the vase in a popcorn tub. Fill the space between the tub and vase with popcorn.

Thanksgiving

Thanksgiving is my favorite holiday. The whole family gathers together, but you don't have the pressure of gift giving, which to me is so very stressful when you have to really think, "What does this person need that they don't have?," because we've got everything we need. In fact, we're all stinking spoiled. So I adore Thanksgiving because it's all about family, it's all about food, and it's all about just being together.

After my mama and daddy died, we spent every Thanksgiving over in Statesboro, Georgia, where my daddy's brother, Uncle Burney, and my Aunt Glynnis lived. I was like a kid waiting on it; I could not hardly wait. We would have the most wonderful time. There were almost thirty people and Uncle Burney would have to go borrow campers from friends 'cause there wasn't enough room in the house. Aunt Jesse was a very good cook, plus we all would bring our favorite dishes. Bubba's wife would bring lasagna and cheesecakes. Our aunt, Beth Hiers, would bring sweet potato pies and fresh vegetables from Uncle Bob's garden. I would always make chicken potpies, some kind of dessert, and the dressing. I've always used the same dressing recipe through the years—I just don't think it can be improved upon.

If you've got a small family, and you don't want to go the turkey route, a roasted hen is wonderful, or a roasted chicken if you're talking about a really small family. Another way to stay in keeping with the Thanksgiving meal, but really downsize, is to go with Cornish game hens.

But no matter what the bird is, for it to be Thanksgiving, I've got to have gravy, I've got to have the dressing, I've got to have fresh green beans, and I've got to have cranberry sauce. I've got to have some kind of dessert with pumpkin in it, whether it's pumpkin trifle or pumpkin gooey butter cakes or pumpkin cheesecake or pumpkin pie.

In 2005, I tried something new: a turducken—a boneless turkey, duck, and chicken tied together and baked with my famous oyster dressing. With Michael, Jamie, and Bobby assisting me, and the rest of my family looking on, that show became one of the Food Network's top-rated shows of all time. And now the whole world knows that while our meal is cooking and my home is taking on all those delicious smells, my family sits around and plays poker! Anyway, I'm giving you some of my treasured recipes in this menu so that your Thanksgiving meal can be as wonderful as ours was that day. I feel so blessed every day. I hope you do, too.

Paula's Pearls of Wisdom

There is nothing that makes my and Michael's heart sing like the love of our children, and there is nothing we love more than seeing them all together, laughing, talking, and gobbling up that delicious Thanksgiving meal.

MENU

Turducken
Brown Gravy
Southern Corn Bread Dressing
Creamy Macaroni and Cheese
Deviled Oysters
Southern Pole Beans
Baked Sweet Potatoes with Butter
and Brown Sugar
Stuffed Cranberry Sauce
Ambrosia
Fresh Apple Cake
Double-Chocolate Cream Pie
Pumpkin Cheesecake

The Next Day
Chicken Potpie

The Next Week
Turkey and Stuffing Casserole

TURDUCKEN

You can order a turducken from the meat department in a large supermarket, or you may order a Cajun-style stuffed turducken from www.turducken.com. You should place your order several weeks in advance. Cooking instructions are included; be prepared to cook the turducken on a baking rack with a pan underneath for about 5 hours. When done, remove the turducken from the oven and place it on a carving board. Pour 3 cups water into the pan drippings in the bottom of the pan and use a wooden spoon to scrape up all of the drippings. This will be used for the brown gravy, below. After removing it from the oven, allow to cool about 15 minutes before carving. Slice thinly—there will be beautiful "ribbons" of the various meats.

One 15-pound turducken will serve about 20

BROWN GRAVY

This is a beautiful caramel color and is yummy poured over the dressing.

4 tablespoons (½ stick) butter
¼ cup all-purpose flour
3 cups pan drippings from the
    turducken or turkey
Salt and pepper

In a 1-quart saucepan over low heat, melt the butter. Whisk in the flour until the mixture is completely smooth. Strain 3 cups of pan drippings (to eliminate lumps) into a measuring cup. Slowly pour the drippings into the flour mixture, stirring constantly to keep the gravy smooth as it thickens over low heat. When it is the desired thickness, taste to see if it needs a little salt or pepper. Turn off the heat and cover the gravy until it is time to use. Reheat and pour into a gravy boat when ready to serve.

Makes 3 cups gravy, enough to serve about 20

SOUTHERN CORN BREAD DRESSING

This is a classic southern soft dressing.

CORN BREAD

2 tablespoons bacon grease or
    vegetable oil
1 cup self-rising cornmeal
½ cup self-rising flour
¾ cup buttermilk
2 eggs

DRESSING

1 recipe Corn Bread, crumbled
4 slices white bread, dried in
    the oven and crumbled
40 (1 sleeve) saltine crackers,
    crumbled
½ cup (1 stick) butter
2 cups chopped celery
1 large yellow onion, chopped
1 teaspoon salt
½ teaspoon pepper
2 teaspoons poultry seasoning
7 cups chicken stock
5 large eggs, beaten

1. Preheat the oven to 400°F. Grease an 8-inch square or round metal pan with the bacon grease or vegetable oil.

2. Combine the cornmeal, flour, buttermilk, and eggs in a 1-quart bowl and mix well with a metal spoon. Pour into the prepared pan and bake for about 20 minutes, until very lightly browned on the top. Remove from the oven and allow to cool in the pan until cool enough to handle. Crumble when cool.

3. In a large bowl, combine the crumbled corn bread, white bread, and saltine crackers. In a 12-inch skillet, melt the butter over low heat. Add the celery and onion and sauté until soft, about 10 minutes. Pour the sautéed vegetables over the corn bread mixture. Add the salt, pepper, and poultry seasoning.

4. About 1½ hours before you want to serve your meal, preheat the oven to 350°F. Spray a 13 by 9-inch baking dish with vegetable oil cooking spray.

5. Add the stock to the corn bread mixture. Stir in the eggs. The mixture will be very soupy. Pour the mixture into the prepared dish. Bake the dressing for 50 minutes, until puffed and lightly browned. Serve with turducken and brown gravy.

Serves about 20

CREAMY MACARONI AND CHEESE

I didn't think my macaroni and cheese could be improved upon, but adding the Cheddar cheese soup gives it a wonderful, creamy texture and helps to "stretch" the dish.

2 cups uncooked elbow
    macaroni (an 8-ounce box
    isn't quite 2 cups)
2½ cups (about 10 ounces)
    grated sharp Cheddar
    cheese
3 eggs, beaten
½ cup sour cream
One 10.75-ounce can
    condensed Cheddar cheese
    soup
4 tablespoons (½ stick) butter,
    cut into pieces
½ teaspoon salt
1 cup whole milk
½ teaspoon dry mustard
½ teaspoon pepper

1. Preheat the oven to 350°F. Spray a 13 by 9-inch baking dish with vegetable oil cooking spray.

2. Boil the macaroni in a 2-quart saucepan in plenty of water until tender, about 7 minutes. Drain. Return the drained macaroni to the saucepan and add 2 cups of the cheese. Stir until the cheese melts while the macaroni is still hot. Add the eggs, sour cream, soup, butter, salt, milk, mustard, and pepper and stir well.

3. Pour the macaroni into the prepared dish. Smooth the top and sprinkle the remaining ½ cup cheese on top. Bake for 40 minutes, until browned and bubbly.

Serves 12

{ Note: The macaroni and cheese can be prepared earlier in the day or the day before and refrigerated unbaked, covered, until needed. Allow to come to room temperature before baking. }

DEVILED OYSTERS

I'm going to admit up front that this isn't a pretty dish. However, it's delicious, and will be the hit of your dinner.

1 pint shucked fresh raw
   oysters
½ cup (1 stick) butter
2 cups finely chopped celery
2 small yellow onions, finely
   chopped
1 clove garlic, minced
3 hard-boiled eggs
4 slices white bread, toasted
   and finely crumbled
¼ cup chopped fresh parsley

1. Preheat the oven to 350°F. Spray a 1½-quart baking dish with vegetable oil cooking spray.

2. Drain the oysters and discard the liquor. If the oysters are small, leave whole. If they are large, snip in two with kitchen shears.

3. In a 10-inch skillet, melt the butter over low heat. Sauté the celery, onions, and garlic until soft, about 10 minutes. Stir in the oysters and sauté for 3 to 4 minutes. Do not overcook.

4. In a medium bowl, mash the eggs with a fork. Add the toast crumbs and parsley. Pour in the sautéed vegetables and oysters. Stir well. Place the oyster mixture into the prepared baking dish. Bake for 20 minutes, until bubbly and lightly browned.

Serves 8 to 10

SOUTHERN POLE BEANS

Pole beans are large, flat green beans adored by southerners. You may substitute green beans if pole beans are unavailable.

3 pounds pole beans, ends
    and strings removed,
    snapped into 3-inch pieces
¼ pound salt pork, sliced thin,
    like bacon
¼ cup bacon grease
2 cups chicken broth
2 teaspoons House Seasoning
    (page 147)

1. Place the beans in a colander, wash, and set aside to drain.

2. In a large cast-iron Dutch oven, lightly brown the salt pork in the bacon grease over medium heat, turning often, for about 10 minutes.

3. Add the pole beans to the pot and toss to coat with the bacon grease. Add the broth and House Seasoning. Cook over medium-low heat, covered tightly, for about 30 minutes (or longer), until the beans are tender and flavorful.

Serves 12

BAKED SWEET POTATOES WITH BUTTER
AND BROWN SUGAR

This is an alternative to the many sweet potato casseroles that are out there.

3 large sweet potatoes
6 tablespoons (¾ stick) butter
3 tablespoons light brown
   sugar

1. Preheat the oven to 350°F. Scrub the outside of the potatoes. Pierce the potatoes in several places with a sharp knife.

2. Place the potatoes in a baking pan and bake until soft, about 1½ hours.

3. When done, make a large slit in each potato and plump up the "meat" inside. Place 2 tablespoons butter and 1 tablespoon brown sugar down into each slit. Quarter the potatoes crosswise and place on a serving dish.

Serves 12

STUFFED CRANBERRY SAUCE

I made this on my show, and I loved it so much, I wanted everyone to have the recipe.

One 8-ounce container
    whipped cream cheese
2 tablespoons mayonnaise
½ cup finely chopped pecans
Two 16-ounce cans jellied
    cranberry sauce, chilled

1. Mix the cream cheese and mayonnaise until creamy. Add the pecans and stir until well mixed.

2. Remove the lids from the cranberry sauce cans. Run a knife around the inside of the cans to loosen the sauce. Slide the cranberry sauce whole from each can. Slice the cranberry sauce into ¼-inch rounds (you will get about 7 to 8 slices per can).

3. Spread the cream cheese mixture on half the rounds and place another round on top, like a sandwich. Cut each round in half and place on a pretty white dish. Cover with plastic wrap. Keep in the refrigerator until ready to serve. This can be made several hours in advance.

Serves 14 to 16

AMBROSIA

love to serve this traditional southern dish for Thanksgiving. Add the bananas at the last minute.

12 medium juice oranges
One 8-ounce can crushed
  pineapple, with juice
One 8-ounce can pineapple
  chunks, with juice
½ cup sweetened flaked
  coconut
¼ cup sugar
One 4-ounce jar maraschino
  cherries, drained and rinsed
½ cup chopped toasted pecans
2 bananas, sliced
1 cup whipping cream,
  whipped with 1 tablespoon
  confectioners' sugar

Peel and section the oranges, removing all the membrane. Place the sections into a large glass bowl. Add the pineapple, coconut, and sugar and stir to combine. Refrigerate until about 30 minutes before serving time. At that time, add the cherries, pecans, and bananas. Stir before serving. Serve with a slotted spoon in dessert dishes with a dollop of sweetened whipped cream, or over pound cake.

Serves 18 to 20

FRESH APPLE CAKE

This gets better the longer it sits, so I suggest making it at least a day in advance.

2 cups plus 3 tablespoons
    sugar

3 teaspoons ground cinnamon

1½ cups vegetable oil

3 large eggs

3 cups chopped Granny Smith
    apples, peeled (about 3
    medium apples)

2 teaspoons vanilla extract

¼ teaspoon freshly grated
    nutmeg

3 cups all-purpose flour

1 teaspoon baking soda

½ teaspoon salt

1 cup chopped pecans

½ cup raisins or coconut, your
    choice (or both!)

1. Preheat the oven to 325°F. Generously grease a 10-inch tube pan. Combine 3 tablespoons of the sugar and 1 teaspoon of the cinnamon and coat the inside of the pan with the mixture by shaking the pan all around until the sides and bottom are coated.

2. Beat the oil and the remaining 2 cups sugar with an electric mixer until well blended. Add the eggs, one at a time, beating well after each addition. With a spatula, stir in the apples and vanilla. Sift together the remaining 2 teaspoons cinnamon, the nutmeg, flour, baking soda, and salt. Add the flour mixture to the apple mixture and mix well with a spatula. Add the pecans and raisins or coconut. The batter will be very thick.

3. Spoon the batter into the prepared pan and smooth the top. Lift the pan from the counter about 2 inches and drop it back down to get out all of the air bubbles.

4. Bake the cake for 1½ to 1¾ hours, until a tester inserted in the center comes out clean. Allow to rest on the countertop for at least 30 minutes before turning out onto a cake plate to cool completely.

Serves 12

DOUBLE-CHOCOLATE CREAM PIE

This is just a good ol' chocolate pie. Have whipped cream and toasted pecans ready to dress it up when it's served.

1 cup sugar
¼ cup cocoa
¼ cup cornstarch
Pinch of salt
3 cups whole milk
3 egg yolks
1½ teaspoons vanilla extract
1 cup semisweet chocolate chips
One 9-inch deep-dish piecrust, baked and cooled
Sweetened whipped cream
Chopped toasted pecans

In a heavy-bottomed 1-quart saucepan, combine the sugar, cocoa, cornstarch, and salt. Stir with a spoon to mix. Combine the milk and egg yolks and whisk until well blended. Slowly begin adding the milk and egg mixture to the chocolate mixture, blending well with a metal spoon. Cook the mixture over medium heat until it thickens, stirring constantly, about 5 minutes. When it is quite thick, add the vanilla and chocolate chips. Stir until completely blended. Pour into the piecrust. Allow to cool, then cover and refrigerate until ready to serve. Serve with plenty of whipped cream and chopped toasted pecans.

Serves 8

PUMPKIN CHEESECAKE

This is very rich and dense—a little sliver is all you need.

1¾ cups graham cracker
   crumbs
2 tablespoons light brown
   sugar
1 teaspoon ground cinnamon
½ cup (1 stick) butter, melted
Three 8-ounce packages
   cream cheese, at room
   temperature
1½ cups granulated sugar
2 tablespoons all-purpose flour
1 teaspoon vanilla extract
⅛ teaspoon freshly grated
   nutmeg
⅛ teaspoon ground cloves
3 large eggs
1 large egg yolk
One 15-ounce can pumpkin
¼ cup sour cream
Whipped cream, for garnish
Toasted pecan halves, for
   garnish

1. Preheat the oven to 350°F. Spray a 9-inch springform pan with vegetable oil cooking spray.

2. Combine the graham cracker crumbs, brown sugar, and ½ teaspoon of the cinnamon in a medium bowl. Pour the melted butter over the mixture and stir until all of the crumbs are moistened. Press this mixture on the bottom and about 1½ inches up the sides of the pan.

3. Beat the cream cheese with an electric mixer until it is very smooth. Add the remaining ½ teaspoon cinnamon, the granulated sugar, flour, vanilla, nutmeg, cloves, eggs, egg yolk, pumpkin, and sour cream and beat at low speed until the mixture is very smooth.

4. Spread the batter in the pan and place the pan on a baking sheet for easier handling. Place the baking sheet in the center of the oven and bake the cheesecake until the center is set, about 1 hour. Cool on a wire rack for 15 minutes.

5. To loosen the cheesecake from the springform pan, run a butter knife along the inside of the pan. Remove the outer ring and allow the cake to cool completely on a wire rack. Cover tightly and refrigerate for at least 4 hours before serving.

6. Bring to room temperature before serving with whipped cream and toasted pecan halves.

Makes 12 to 14 servings

CHICKEN POTPIE

This dish is a labor of love. For many years, this was the dish I was asked to bring to Thanksgiving gatherings, not for the Thanksgiving meal, but for the days afterward when the thought of another turkey sandwich made everyone feel ill. This is rich, delicious, and beautiful. I have always layered my dough throughout the potpie and finished off the top with a lattice crust. The dough absorbs all those delicious flavors—yum!

One 4- to 5-pound chicken, washed under cold water and patted dry

2½ teaspoons salt

½ teaspoon pepper

3 cups all-purpose flour

¼ teaspoon baking powder

¾ cup vegetable shortening

3 to 4 tablespoons ice water

One 8.25-ounce can sliced carrots, drained

½ a 10-ounce package frozen green peas

4 cups chicken broth (from cooking the chicken)

1. In a 4-quart stockpot, place the chicken in 4 cups water. Add 1½ teaspoons of the salt and the pepper. Bring the water to a rolling boil, then reduce the heat and simmer the chicken over medium heat until it is very tender, 50 minutes to 1 hour. Cool to room temperature. Remove the chicken from the broth and pick the meat from the bones, leaving the meat in large pieces. Discard the skin and bones and set aside the meat.

2. Sift together the flour, the remaining 1 teaspoon salt, and the baking powder. Place in a food processor. Add the shortening and pulse until the shortening is completely incorporated. Add the ice water, 1 tablespoon at a time, and pulse until the mixture holds together into a ball.

3. Divide the ball of dough in two, with one ball larger than the other. Roll out the smaller ball about ¼ inch thick and cut into strips.

4. Lay half of the chicken in a 13 by 9-inch baking dish. Distribute half of the carrots and half of the peas over the chicken. Top with strips of unbaked dough. Top with the remaining chicken, carrots, and peas. Pour the broth into the casserole until it reaches the top of the chicken.

5. Roll out the larger ball of dough about ¼ inch thick and cut it into strips. Use these strips to form a lattice crust over the chicken potpie. At this point, the dish can be refrigerated, covered, for up to 24 hours.

6. Preheat the oven to 350°F. Remove the potpie from the refrigerator and place on a baking sheet to

make it easier to transfer to and from the oven. Bake for 1 hour, until the crust begins to brown and the pie is bubbly. Serve warm.

Makes 8 servings

TURKEY AND STUFFING CASSEROLE

When you finish your meal, get one of your kitchen helpers to slice the turkey so that you'll have plenty of meat for sandwiches for the weekend. Cube and freeze what is left so that you can make this casserole sometime when you're in need of something quick and easy. It won't win any James Beard awards, but it will give your turkey a fresh look.

4 to 5 cups diced leftover turkey
One 10.75-ounce can condensed cream of mushroom soup
One 8-ounce carton sour cream
3 cups herb-flavored stuffing mix (I like Pepperidge Farm)
½ cup (1 stick) butter, melted
1 cup chicken broth (canned is fine)

1. Preheat the oven to 350°F. Spray a 13 by 9-inch glass casserole dish with vegetable oil cooking spray.

2. In a medium bowl, stir together the turkey, soup, and sour cream.

3. Place the mixture in the prepared dish and pat down evenly with the back of a spoon.

4. In a clean medium bowl, stir together the stuffing mix, butter, and broth. Spread evenly over the turkey mixture.

5. Bake for 30 to 40 minutes, until the stuffing topping is browned and the casserole is hot and bubbly.

Serves 8

❖ BRANDON'S DECORATING TIPS ❖

Use miniature pumpkins or beautiful fall leaves as place cards and write your guests' names on them with a paint pen. I like to take miniature Indian corn, tie three cobs together with raffia, and use them as napkin rings. A simple way to welcome your guests is to take brown paper bags, fill them with sand, and place a votive light in each one. Line the driveway with them and light them just before your guests arrive. It's amazing how wonderful they look.

Sunday Afternoon Football Party

You know, I think there's nothing that the men in my family like any better than watching football. Well, Michael enjoys it, but my sons, Jamie and Bobby, and my brother, Bubba, adore a good football game. In fact, Jamie and Bobby are such big Georgia football fans that Bobby wound up giving his brother a bulldog who is a great-grandson of UGA, the mascot of the University of Georgia team. His name is Champ and he is precious.

Right before they were married, Jamie and his wife, Brooke, bought a house. It just so happens that this house has a guesthouse. Well, Jamie has turned that guesthouse into what he calls the Dawg House—and I could not believe the other day when I

Brooke and Jamie.

went in there, this room is decorated so cute, all filled with Georgia memorabilia. The guesthouse has a kitchen, it has a living room, it has a bathroom, and it has a bedroom. Brooke took the bedroom; the Georgia stuff is not allowed in the bedroom. In the living room, where they have the TV, this room is strictly all about football.

Bobby, my other son, who is maybe almost equally as crazy about the Dawgs as Jamie is, just splurged on a fabulous item for his new home: a full-size movie screen. He pushes a button and it comes down from the ceiling. Well, do I have to tell you how those guys love watching football on that screen?

But not only is football important, the food is also very important. You can't watch a game and not have a cold beer and something good to eat. We've included quite a variety in this meal—corn chowder for the lighter eaters, a hearty taco soup, two kinds of chicken wings with a delicious blue cheese dip, a pretty pink shrimp dip, and a twist on a favorite combo—hamburgers and onion rings. And no gathering of mine would be complete without something sweet—one of my famous gooey butter cakes seemed perfect with this hearty menu.

Paula's Pearls of Wisdom
Remember, girls, a good football game allows
you some quality time just to yourself.
I promise the men won't miss you.

CORN CHOWDER

What can beat the taste of chowder made with fresh sweet corn cut from the cob? This is heavenly, and would make a perfect summer lunch. Corn is still available in southern groceries in the fall.

2 tablespoons butter

1 cup chopped yellow onion

½ cup chopped celery

2 baking potatoes, peeled and diced

4 cups chicken broth (homemade or canned)

4 ears white or yellow corn on the cob

1. In a heavy-bottomed 4-quart stockpot, melt the butter over medium heat. Add the onion, celery, and potatoes and sauté for about 2 minutes. Add the broth and boil the vegetables over medium-high heat for about 15 minutes, until the potatoes are very soft.

2. Meanwhile, cut the corn from the cobs with a sharp knife; place each corncob in the middle of a large bowl to catch the kernels and juice.

½ cup half-and-half

½ teaspoon salt

¼ teaspoon pepper

One 10.75-ounce can condensed cream of celery soup

¼ cup chopped red bell pepper

3. Add the corn to the soup and cook for 5 minutes more. Add the half-and-half, salt, pepper, and the cream of celery soup. Stir well to combine. Simmer until hot. Serve immediately. Garnish with the bell pepper.

Makes about 6 cups: 6 appetizer servings or 3 main-dish servings

TACO SOUP

You literally just brown the meat and dump in cans of beans, tomatoes, and corn to make this soup. The package of taco seasoning mix does all the seasoning and thickening for you!

1¾ pounds ground chuck

1 large yellow onion, chopped

2 cloves garlic, minced

Two 14.5-ounce cans diced tomatoes, with juice

One 15- to 16-ounce can kidney beans, drained

One 15- to 16-ounce can pinto beans, drained

One 15- to 16-ounce can black beans, drained

One 15.25-ounce can whole kernel corn, drained

One 14.5-ounce can chicken broth

One 1.25-ounce package taco seasoning mix

1. In a large Dutch oven, cook the beef, onion, and garlic over medium-high heat until browned, stirring until the meat crumbles. Drain well and return the meat and vegetables to the Dutch oven.

2. Stir in the tomatoes, beans, corn, broth, and seasoning mix. Bring to a boil, reduce the heat, and simmer, uncovered, for 30 minutes.

Serves 10 to 12

CHILI-CHEESE CORN MUFFINS

These are so yummy with the soups.

1¾ cups self-rising yellow
  cornmeal
1 cup all-purpose flour
¼ cup sugar
1 cup (¼ pound) shredded
  sharp Cheddar cheese
¼ cup seeded and chopped
  poblano pepper
1½ cups whole milk
¾ cup (1½ sticks) butter,
  melted
2 large eggs, lightly beaten

1. Preheat the oven to 400°F. Spray muffin tins with vegetable oil cooking spray.

2. In a large bowl, combine the cornmeal, flour, sugar, cheese, and poblano pepper. Make a well in the center of the mixture. In a small bowl, combine the milk, butter, and eggs. Add the wet ingredients to the dry ingredients all at once, stirring with a spoon just until moistened. Spoon the batter into the prepared muffin tins, filling each cup about three-quarters full. Bake for 20 minutes, until the muffins are lightly browned and set.

Makes 18 muffins

TERIYAKI AND BUFFALO CHICKEN WINGS

Serve the wings with celery sticks and Blue Cheese Dressing (opposite).

36 fresh or frozen chicken
    wings, tips trimmed
Salt and pepper
Vegetable oil, for deep frying

TERIYAKI SAUCE

½ cup soy sauce
3 tablespoons light brown
    sugar
3 cloves garlic, minced
1 teaspoon grated fresh ginger
2 tablespoons dry sherry

BUFFALO SAUCE

4 tablespoons (½ stick) butter,
    melted
2 tablespoons hot sauce
1 teaspoon red wine vinegar

1. Thaw the frozen wings under running water until the glaze has melted. Dry the wings thoroughly. Salt and pepper to taste.

2. In a Dutch oven or an electric frying pan, pour in 3 inches of oil and heat to 360°F. Using tongs, lower each wing individually into the oil. Fry until the wings are crisp and brown, about 12 to 14 minutes. Drain on paper towels. You will have to cook the wings in several batches. This can be done several hours before the party. Leave at room temperature, covered loosely with foil, after they have cooled completely.

3. Preheat the oven to 350°F.

4. Combine the teriyaki sauce ingredients in a small measuring cup. Combine the Buffalo sauce ingredients in another small measuring cup. Place 18 wings in one baking dish and the remaining 18 wings in another baking dish. Pour the teriyaki sauce on the wings in one dish and toss to coat. Pour the Buffalo sauce on the other wings and toss to coat. Place in the oven for about 5 minutes, until the sauces have glazed the wings and the wings are heated through.

Serves 6

BLUE CHEESE DRESSING

Have plenty of fresh celery sticks on hand.

½ cup mayonnaise
½ cup sour cream
½ cup (about 2 ounces)
   crumbled blue cheese

Stir all of the ingredients together. Keep covered in the refrigerator until serving time.

Makes 1½ cups

PINK SHRIMP DIP

I like dips on game day. This one has a great flavor and a beautiful pink color. Serve it with corn chips.

Two 8-ounce packages cream
   cheese, at room
   temperature
2 teaspoons prepared
   horseradish
Dash of Worcestershire sauce
½ cup seafood cocktail sauce
   (bottled sauce or
   homemade, using recipe on
   page 150)
1 pound shrimp, boiled,
   peeled, deveined, and
   coarsely chopped

Combine the cream cheese, horseradish, Worcestershire sauce, and cocktail sauce in a medium bowl. Blend well. Stir in the shrimp. Refrigerate, covered, until serving time.

Serves 12 to 16

JAMIE'S CHEESEBURGER PIES

Jamie made these on my Food Network Thanksgiving special. They are oh so good!

1 pound lean ground beef

½ cup finely diced Vidalia onion or other sweet onion

1 teaspoon Montreal Steak Seasoning

1 tablespoon Dale's Steak Seasoning Sauce (available from www.dalesseasoning.com)

5 slices cheese, American, Swiss, or sharp Cheddar

1 sheet frozen puff pastry dough, allowed to sit at room temperature for about 20 minutes

1 egg yolk

1. Preheat the oven to 375°F. Prepare the grill.

2. Mix the ground beef, onion, steak seasoning, and seasoning sauce together (using your hands is the most efficient way to do this). Form into 5 small flat patties. Grill the hamburgers to medium-well. (You may also panfry the patties.) Remove from the grill and top each burger with a slice of cheese.

3. Roll the puff pastry sheet to flatten slightly. Eyeball the sheet and cut it into 5 relatively even rectangles. They don't have to be exact.

4. Cover each burger with a piece of puff pastry and wrap it around the bottom, pinching all of the edges to seal. Place on an ungreased baking sheet, pinched side down.

5. Whisk together the egg yolk and 1 teaspoon water to make an egg wash. Brush each wrapped pastry with the egg wash. Bake for about 15 minutes, until the puff pastry is nice and brown.

Serves 5

FRIED ONION RINGS WITH CHILI SAUCE

Lots of people double-dip their onion rings in egg and then in flour. I like 'em just as well with just a dusting of flour, and it's a lot less messy.

CHILI SAUCE

1 cup mayonnaise

3 tablespoons chili sauce

1 teaspoon chili powder

⅛ teaspoon cayenne pepper

ONION RINGS

2 medium white or yellow
  onions

1 teaspoon seasoned salt

2 cups all-purpose flour

Vegetable oil, for deep frying

Salt

1. To make the chili sauce, combine the mayonnaise, chili sauce, chili powder, and cayenne in a small bowl and stir well. Cover and chill until serving time. Makes about 1 cup.

2. Slice the onions into very thin rings and separate the rings. Spread them out and sprinkle with seasoned salt. Place the flour in a resealable plastic bag. Put the onion rings in the bag in batches, close tightly, and shake until the onion rings are coated.

3. Pour the oil into a Dutch oven and heat to 360°F. Fry the onion rings in batches for 3 to 4 minutes, until they are brown and crispy. Remove with tongs and drain on paper towels. Taste and salt if necessary. Serve with the chili sauce.

Serves about 6

TOFFEE GOOEY BUTTER CAKE

Here's yet another *gooey butter cake recipe! There are almost endless varieties, but no two taste alike.*

CAKE

One 18.25-ounce package
   yellow cake mix
1 large egg
½ cup (1 stick) butter, melted

FILLING

One 8-ounce package cream
   cheese, softened
2 large eggs
1 teaspoon vanilla extract
One 1-pound box
   confectioners' sugar
½ cup (1 stick) butter, melted
1 cup almond or chocolate
   toffee bits

1. Preheat the oven to 350°F. Spray a 13 by 9 by 2-inch baking pan with vegetable oil cooking spray.

2. Make the cake: In the bowl of an electric mixer at medium speed, combine the cake mix, egg, and butter and mix well. Pat evenly into the bottom of the prepared baking pan and set aside.

3. Make the filling: In the same bowl you used for the cake, beat the cream cheese at medium speed until it is smooth. Beat in the eggs and vanilla. Add the confectioners' sugar and beat again at low speed until blended. Add the butter. Mix well. Fold in the toffee bits with a spatula.

4. Pour the filling over the cake mixture and spread it evenly. Bake for 40 to 50 minutes; the center should be just a little bit gooey. Remove from the oven and allow to cool completely. Cut into pieces.

Makes 24 servings

❖ BRANDON'S DECORATING TIPS ❖

This is a casual party, and I'd keep it simple. Line tin buckets with your local paper's sports pages; fill two with wings and another with chips. Fill a larger bucket with ice and place the soft drinks and beer in there.

Homemade Christmas Gifts

*Y*ou know, sometimes you really don't realize what an impression a home-made gift makes on somebody. Jamie told me one day, "Mama, do you remember when at Christmastime, you'd go out and buy those little glass jars and you'd fill 'em with all your homemade candy and put a ribbon on 'em and that would be my gift to my teachers? I would be so proud. I remember my chest puffing out when the teacher would say, 'Jamie, thank you so much. That was the most wonderful candy I've ever eaten.' Mama," he said, "you will never, never know how proud those homemade candies made me feel."

When you don't have much money, a simple gift of food delivered in a brown paper bag that you have sponge-painted with a Christmas tree or holly leaf can send such a personal message of sharing and caring. I've chosen a few recipes that even children can do—they can certainly be taught to measure out the ingredients for the fruited rice curry or the lemon-dill rice mixes or the spiced tea mix. Any of these would make such wonderful teacher gifts, and would provide welcome relief from the traditional coffee mug! For your salad-loving friends, give the Greek salad dressing in a small carafe, and those with a sweet tooth will appreciate the peppermint bark or the pretzel-peanut bark. A small tin of cheese straws is always welcome for an afternoon nibble. As for the fruitcake, well, I think fruitcake gets a bad rap. My grandmother always made a fruitcake for the holidays, placing a small open container of brandy in the center of the cake. The cake would absorb the brandy flavor as it aged. By the time you ate the last slice, it would knock your socks off! Now, that's a gift worth getting! Happy gift giving!

Paula's Pearls of Wisdom

Anyone can go to a store and buy a gift,
but it's a special person who gives their time to create one.

Fruited Rice Curry Mix
Lemon-Dill Rice Mix
Russian Spiced Tea Mix
Greek Salad Dressing
Peppermint Bark
Pretzel-Peanut Bark
Cheese Straws
Oven Caramel Corn
Icebox Fruitcake
Orange-Ginger Butter
Cinnamon-Honey Butter
Herb Butter

FRUITED RICE CURRY MIX

This goes well with roast pork or chicken.

1¼ cups raw white rice

2 teaspoons curry powder

2 beef bouillon cubes, crushed, or 2 teaspoons granulated bouillon

½ teaspoon salt

¼ cup slivered almonds

2 tablespoons golden raisins

¼ cup chopped dried mixed fruit

Combine all of the ingredients in a small bowl and mix well with your fingers. Place the mixture in a sandwich-size resealable plastic bag and attach this recipe: Combine the contents of this package with 2½ cups water and 2 tablespoons butter in a 2-quart saucepan. Bring to a boil, cover, reduce the heat to low, and simmer for 20 minutes. Makes 3 cups, about 6 servings.

LEMON-DILL RICE MIX

This is particularly good with seafood, although I also like it with baked chicken.

1½ teaspoons grated lemon zest, dried

½ teaspoon dried minced onion

2 chicken bouillon cubes, crushed, or 2 teaspoons granulated bouillon

1 teaspoon dried dill weed

½ teaspoon salt

1¼ cups raw white rice

Combine all of the ingredients in a small bowl and mix well. Place the mixture in a sandwich-size resealable plastic bag and attach this recipe: Bring 2½ cups water and 1 tablespoon butter to a boil in a 2-quart saucepan. Add the contents of this package. Reduce the heat to low, cover, and simmer for 20 minutes. Makes 3 cups, about 6 servings.

RUSSIAN SPICED TEA MIX

This is fun for really young children. They can measure and mix the ingredients, and could even be invited to "tea" by the recipient!

One 3-ounce jar Lipton
   Sweetened Iced Tea Mix
One 21.1-ounce container
   Tang
1 tablespoon ground
   cinnamon
1 tablespoon freshly grated
   nutmeg
1 tablespoon ground allspice

Combine all of the ingredients in a medium bowl and mix well with a metal spoon. Store in small plastic containers or glass jars with tight-fitting lids. Attach this recipe: Use 2 heaping teaspoons in 6 ounces of hot water for hot tea or 2 heaping teaspoons in 6 ounces of cold water for a refreshing summer beverage over ice.

Makes 5 cups, about 60 servings

GREEK SALAD DRESSING

By all means include the recipe; your friends are going to want to keep this on hand at all times in the fridge. After you shake the dressing, pour it into an attractive bottle (or bottles) with a stopper.

½ cup olive oil

¼ cup canola oil

⅓ cup fresh lemon juice (about 3 lemons)

1 teaspoon salt

¼ teaspoon pepper

1 clove garlic, minced

¾ teaspoon dried oregano

¼ teaspoon sugar

Place all of the ingredients in a pint jar with a tight-fitting lid. Shake well. Store in the refrigerator. When ready to use, allow the dressing to come to room temperature and shake well.

Makes a little more than 1 cup

PEPPERMINT BARK

The weekend when I was walking the red carpet for the screening of Elizabethtown *(the movie I appeared in with Orlando Bloom and Kirsten Dunst), I had time to teach actress Judy Greer how to make this simple but delicious candy. Package it in Chinese food take-out cartons for individual gifts.*

Peppermint candy canes
18 squares white chocolate
   (1 ounce each)
Peppermint extract (optional)

1. Line a rimmed cookie sheet with parchment or waxed paper. Place the candy canes in a heavy-duty plastic bag and hammer into ¼-inch chunks or smaller. You should have about 1 cup.

2. Melt the chocolate in a double boiler over simmering water until smooth, or melt in the microwave in a 2-quart glass dish. Microwave on high (100%) for 1 minute, stir, and microwave on high for 10 seconds more. If necessary, microwave on high for an additional 10 seconds, and stir until the chocolate is melted and smooth.

3. Combine the candy cane chunks with the melted chocolate. Add 1 drop of peppermint extract, if desired. Pour the mixture onto the prepared cookie sheet and place in the refrigerator for 45 minutes or until firm. Remove from the cookie sheet and break the bark into irregular pieces, like peanut brittle.

Makes about 6 cups

PRETZEL-PEANUT BARK

This is terribly yummy.

18 squares white chocolate
(1 ounce each)
3 cups skinny pretzel sticks,
broken into small pieces but
not crushed, then measured
2 cups dry salted peanuts

1. Line a rimmed cookie sheet with parchment or waxed paper.

2. Melt the chocolate in a double boiler over simmering water until smooth, or melt in the microwave in a 2-quart glass dish. Microwave on high (100%) for 1 minute, stir, and microwave on high for 10 seconds more. If necessary, microwave on high for an additional 10 seconds, and stir until the chocolate is melted and smooth. Stir in the pretzel pieces and peanuts. Stir well with a flexible spatula.

3. Spoon onto the prepared cookie sheet, spreading the mixture out so that the ingredients are relatively evenly distributed.

4. Allow the chocolate to cool for several hours or refrigerate for 45 minutes or until firm. Break the bark into irregular pieces, like peanut brittle. Store in cookie tins, or package in Chinese food take-out cartons lined with waxed paper.

Makes about 8 cups

CHEESE STRAWS

It's important to bake these on an ungreased cookie sheet, not a nonstick sheet or parchment. That way, the bottoms get crisp. It's also important to allow the butter and cheese to come to room temperature.

2 cups self-rising flour

¼ teaspoon cayenne pepper

¼ teaspoon salt

1 cup (2 sticks) butter, at room temperature

2 cups (½ pound) grated sharp Cheddar cheese, at room temperature

1. Preheat the oven to 350°F.

2. Sift together the flour, cayenne, and salt and set aside. Using an electric mixer, cream together the butter and cheese until blended. Add the flour mixture slowly, beating at low speed, then continue to beat for 5 minutes, until very creamy, scraping down the sides of the bowl several times.

3. Using a cookie press with a star tip, make 3-inch-long cheese straws, leaving at least ½ inch between each on an ungreased cookie sheet. Bake for 12 minutes. Remove from the oven and allow the straws to sit on the cookie sheet for 5 minutes. Transfer the cheese straws to a wire rack to cool completely. Store in airtight containers.

Makes about 6 dozen

OVEN CARAMEL CORN

This is positively addictive. Put about 2 cups in a clear plastic bag and tie with a beautiful Christmas bow.

7 to 8 quarts popped popcorn
2 cups unsalted peanuts,
    shelled pumpkinseeds,
    and/or sunflower seeds
1 cup light brown sugar
1 cup (2 sticks) butter or
    margarine
1 teaspoon salt
½ cup light corn syrup
1 teaspoon maple-flavored
    pancake syrup
1 teaspoon vanilla extract
1 teaspoon baking soda

1. Preheat the oven to 250°F. Spray rimmed cookie sheets or jelly-roll pans with vegetable oil cooking spray.

2. Place the popcorn and your choice of nuts and/or seeds into a very large bowl. In a medium saucepan, combine the sugar, butter, salt, syrups, and vanilla. Bring to a boil over medium-high heat and continue boiling for 5 minutes, stirring constantly. Remove from the heat and add the baking soda. The mixture will bubble up. Stir vigorously until the mixture is smooth.

3. Pour the hot syrup over the popcorn mix. Stir until the popcorn is coated. This is messy; take your time and use a long-handled spoon.

4. Spread the coated popcorn in the prepared pans. Bake for 1 hour, stirring several times. The mixture will be very sticky.

5. Remove the popcorn from the oven and allow to cool for 15 minutes. Break big hunks apart while the mixture is cooling. When cooled, the sugars will have candy-coated the popcorn. Store in large, airtight plastic containers.

Makes 7 to 8 quarts

ICEBOX FRUITCAKE

What are the holidays without fruitcake? I don't make traditional fruitcake like my grandmother made. Instead, I make this unbelievably easy stir-together fruitcake and put it into mini loaf pans for gift giving. This recipe appeared in The Lady & Sons Just Desserts, *but I wanted you to have it again in case you missed it!*

One 14-ounce can sweetened condensed milk

One 16-ounce bag miniature marshmallows

One 16-ounce box graham crackers, crushed to crumbs

4 cups chopped pecans

One 3.5-ounce can flaked coconut (1⅓ cups)

Two 8-ounce packages chopped dates

One 16-ounce jar maraschino cherries, well drained, halved

½ cup bourbon

1. Spray 10 mini loaf pans with vegetable oil cooking spray.

2. In a 2-quart saucepan, heat the milk and marshmallows together over low heat. Stir constantly (condensed milk scorches easily!) until the marshmallows are melted. Remove the mixture from the heat. Combine the cracker crumbs, pecans, coconut, dates, and cherries in a large bowl. Add the bourbon to the milk mixture and pour over the crumb mixture. Mix well with your hands. Scoop the mixture into the prepared pans and press down firmly to mold into shape. Refrigerate for 2 days or longer before serving.

Makes 10 mini loaves

Someone gave me little baby food jars filled with these flavored butters, and I loved the idea so much, I wanted to pass it along to you!

ORANGE-GINGER BUTTER

This is terrific with coffee cake or muffins, and is also delicious smeared on broiled fish.

½ cup (1 stick) butter, softened
3 tablespoons orange
    marmalade
¼ teaspoon grated fresh
    ginger (the kind in the jar is
    fine)

Combine the ingredients in a small bowl. Pack into a small crock or baby food jar with a decorative lid. Or roll in waxed paper into a log and twist the ends. Chill thoroughly. Wrap in colorful paper.

Makes about ¾ cup

CINNAMON-HONEY BUTTER

I served this the morning after Christmas on homemade waffles.

½ cup (1 stick) butter, softened
2 tablespoons honey
½ teaspoon ground cinnamon

Combine the ingredients in a small bowl. Pack into a small crock or baby food jar with a decorative lid. Or roll in waxed paper into a log and twist the ends. Chill thoroughly. Wrap in colorful paper.

Makes about ½ cup

HERB BUTTER

Delicious on homemade bread. Killer slathered over grilled steak or chicken.

½ (1 stick) butter, softened
1 clove garlic, minced
1 teaspoon dried parsley
   flakes
½ teaspoon dried basil
½ teaspoon dried thyme

Combine the ingredients in a small bowl. Pack into a small crock or baby food jar with a decorative lid. Or roll in waxed paper into a log and twist the ends. Chill thoroughly. Wrap in colorful paper.

Makes about ½ cup

❖ BRANDON'S DECORATING TIPS ❖

When giving gifts, use everyday objects in unexpected ways. Take some silk fabric and cut it into squares with pinking shears. Place the gift in the middle, then draw up the four corners and tie with a bow. Put cookies or cheese straws on a pretty antique plate and wrap securely with plastic wrap. Tie up the plate with a pretty ribbon and tuck a sprig of greenery—cedar, magnolia, wax myrtle, or boxwood—into the bow.

CHRISTMAS

Christmas has always been my favorite time of year. When Bobby and I were younger, we had a special calendar for December, and every day we took down a candy cane and split it, taking us one day closer to Christmas. The excitement was so high by the 24th, we barely slept. Mom and Dad had a rule that we couldn't go to the Christmas tree until they were up; we did that as a family. My mom always loved to share our thrill as we explored what Santa had left behind. Well, I bet for ten or twelve years our folks didn't log five hours sleep on any Christmas Eve!

Mom always had a special breakfast made the night before; the mornings we spent together with wrapping paper scattered to kingdom come and a belly full of breakfast were just the best.

And then we got older. Dammit.

We started The Bag Lady, a lunch delivery business, in 1989, and for a long time Christmas meant a break from our endless schedule. We were so busy, that one year Mom said we couldn't afford and had no time to get a Christmas tree. I could not face the holidays without that simplest of pleasures. The smell of a fresh-cut tree is one of my favorite things, and while I didn't have the money either, we did have a coat rack. So that was it. I strung that rack with a strand of lights and hung a few glass balls from it. One of the most depressing images from my past has grown to be one of my fondest memories.

Now I am married, and Brooke and I have started our own Christmas traditions. Her family came to visit in 2005, and we spent Christmas morning together surrounded by endless mounds of crumpled wrapping paper . . . and I did the cooking. We so look forward to future Christmases when we hang a special calendar for our children to come. And to losing sleep on Christmas Eve.

Jamie Deen

Christmas Dinner

My family and I just love Christmas. It's all about family, food, and fun to us. We don't have any children running around (yet!), but Christmas 2005 had to be one of the most exciting Christmases in recent history. That was because my niece, Corrie Hiers, helped me select the perfect gift to give her daddy, my brother, Bubba Hiers, and we managed to pull off this surprise together, with the help of Bubba's fiancée, Dawn. Bubba wanted a dog, and I was able to find a chocolate Lab puppy in Atlanta. We met the people halfway, picked up the puppy, and managed to hide him from Bubba until Christmas morning. I put a note on his collar that said, "Hi, I'm not sure what my name is, but I know my daddy's name is Bubba. Would you please help me find him?" Well, Bubba was in a state of shock; he couldn't believe that beautiful puppy was his. You couldn't slap the grin off Bubba's face all day long. Well, he named his puppy UB, after Uncle Bubba's, and UB is now Uncle Bubba's very best friend. Do you know how exciting it is to give somebody a gift that they want so badly? For Corrie, Dawn, and me, giving Bubba that dog was giving ourselves the greatest gift by bringing pleasure to him.

I don't do a lot of variations on my Christmas Day meal. At my house, we are full up with turkey and ham from Thanksgiving, and at the restaurant, we have to cook so many turkeys and hams for Thanksgiving, and throw so many parties with turkey and dressing, that I am just sick to death of turkey by the time Christmas rolls around. All I want is beef. My favorite is the standing rib roast, but let me tell you something: I won't throw away a beef tenderloin, either. And naturally, you have to have a tater—a tater's got to be invited to the table in some shape, form, or fashion.

Paula's Pearls of Wisdom

You know how people are at Christmastime—always doing things for other people? Wouldn't it be great if we kept the spirit of Christmas in our hearts all year?

CRANBERRY HOLIDAY BRIE

This is one of those dishes that is just beautiful to see. When you bring it to the table, the puff pastry dough is browned and beautiful, and then, when you slice into the cheese, the Brie oozes out and the cranberries peek through. The white on red makes this a perfect dish for the holidays—any occasion between Thanksgiving and Valentine's!

1 sheet (½ package) frozen
   puff pastry dough
1 egg
¾ cup apricot preserves
2 tablespoons orange juice
⅓ cup dried cranberries
¼ cup toasted sliced almonds
1 Brie cheese, about 13
   ounces
Water crackers

1. Allow the pastry sheet to thaw in the package about 30 minutes, until pliable. Preheat the oven to 400°F. In a small bowl, beat the egg with 1 teaspoon water to make an egg wash. Set aside.

2. Lightly flour a large wooden cutting board and roll out the pastry dough into a 14-inch square. Cut off the corners to make a circle. Save the extra dough to cut into decorative shapes for a garnish. Spread the apricot preserves on the pastry, leaving a 2-inch margin all around the edge.

3. Pour the orange juice into a small glass dish and add the cranberries, allowing them to absorb the flavor of the orange juice for about 5 minutes, until the cranberries are soft. Drain the cranberries. Arrange the cranberries evenly on top of the apricot preserves. Arrange the almonds evenly on the cranberries. Place the Brie on top of the almonds. Brush the edges of the puff pastry with the egg wash. Completely seal the Brie in the puff pastry. Seal the edges by brushing the egg wash on one edge, as if you are gluing the edges together.

4. Spray a baking sheet with vegetable oil cooking spray. Place the Brie seam side down on the sheet. Decorate the top with pastry cutouts, rerolling scraps of dough, if desired. Brush the top with the remaining egg wash.

5. Bake for 20 minutes. Allow to sit for at least 30 minutes before serving; the cheese will be runny if you cut it too early! Serve with crackers.

Serves 12

STANDING RIB ROAST

This recipe is one of my family's favorites. You can start it early in the day, and finish it when it's time for dinner.

One 5-pound standing rib roast, bone in
1 tablespoon House Seasoning (page 147)

1. Allow the roast to stand at room temperature for at least 1 hour. Preheat the oven to 375°F.

2. Rub the roast with House Seasoning. Place the roast on a rack in a roasting pan with the rib side down and the fatty side up. Roast for 1 hour. Turn off the oven and leave the roast in the oven; do not open the door. About 1 hour and 10 minutes before serving time, turn the oven on to 375°F and reheat the roast for 30 to 40 minutes. Do not remove the roast or reopen the oven door from the time the roast is put in until the final roasting. Remove the roast from the oven and tent with foil. Allow the meat to rest for 25 to 30 minutes before carving.

Serves 8 to 10

SOY-RUBBED TENDERLOIN

This is really so simple. I buy a whole tenderloin when it goes on sale and have it cut in two. I fix one that night and freeze the other for a special occasion.

One 4- to 5-pound beef
    tenderloin
½ cup soy sauce
Freshly ground black pepper

1. Allow the beef to stand at room temperature for 1 hour. Preheat the oven to 425°F.

2. Place the tenderloin in a 13 by 9-inch glass baking dish and rub all over with the soy sauce. Rub the meat all over with a generous amount of black pepper.

3. Roast the tenderloin for 45 to 50 minutes, depending on the degree of doneness you prefer. (Using a meat thermometer, 125°F is rare; 135°F is medium rare; and 140° is medium.) Remove from the oven and allow the meat to rest for 15 minutes before you slice it.

Serves 10 to 12

TWICE-BAKED POTATO CASSEROLE

There just isn't any better combination than meat and potatoes. This is such a great dish because you can make it the day ahead and you've still got that delicious flavor of baked potatoes.

8 medium baking potatoes, about 4 pounds

One 8-ounce package cream cheese, at room temperature

½ cup (1 stick) butter, softened

2 cups (½ pound) shredded sharp Cheddar cheese

1 pint sour cream

2 cloves garlic, minced

1½ teaspoons salt

½ teaspoon pepper

¼ cup chopped chives, for garnish

6 slices bacon, cooked crisp, drained, and crumbled, for garnish

1. Preheat the oven to 350°F. Pierce the potatoes and place on a baking pan. Bake the potatoes for 1 hour and 15 minutes, until very soft.

2. Peel and mash the potatoes in a large bowl with a potato masher or the back of a fork. Add the cream cheese, butter, 1 cup of the Cheddar cheese, and the sour cream. Stir well. Add the garlic, salt, and pepper and stir again.

3. Spray a 13 by 9-inch baking dish with vegetable oil cooking spray. Place the potatoes into the dish. The casserole may now be covered with plastic wrap and refrigerated until ready to bake.

4. When ready to bake, preheat the oven to 350°F. Remove the plastic wrap and bake the potatoes for 30 to 35 minutes, until hot. Sprinkle the remaining 1 cup Cheddar cheese over the top of the casserole and return to the oven for about 5 minutes, until the cheese melts. Garnish with the chopped chives and crumbled bacon before serving.

Serves 10 to 12

BRUSSELS SPROUTS WITH ONION AND BACON

My family really loves my green beans (page 170), and they certainly would work with this menu. But instead I decided that brussels sprouts, which taste and look like sweet little cabbages, would be the right side here.

½ pound lean bacon, finely
   diced
1 cup diced yellow onion
2 cloves garlic, minced
2 pounds brussels sprouts,
   trimmed
2 cups chicken broth
4 tablespoons (½ stick) butter

1. In a heavy-bottomed pot over medium heat, fry the bacon until crisp. Remove the bacon and drain on paper towels.

2. Sauté the onion and garlic in the bacon grease over low heat until soft, about 3 minutes. Add the brussels sprouts and stir them around so that they are coated with the bacon grease.

3. Add the broth and cook, covered, over low heat until the sprouts are easily pierced with a fork, about 12 to 15 minutes. Stir in the butter just before serving. Garnish each serving with bacon bits.

Serves 8

COCONUT POUND CAKE WITH 7-MINUTE FROSTING

I always make a coconut cake for Christmas, always frosted with this fluffy frosting or with whipped cream and coconut, and decorated with holly sprigs.

2 cups (4 sticks) butter, at room temperature

2 cups sugar

2 cups all-purpose flour

6 eggs

One 7-ounce package sweetened flaked coconut (2⅔ cups)

1 teaspoon vanilla extract

GLAZE

1 cup sugar

1 teaspoon coconut extract

7-Minute Frosting (page 212)

1. Preheat the oven to 350°F. Generously grease and flour a 10-inch springform tube pan.

2. Cream the butter and sugar with an electric mixer. Add 1 cup of the flour and mix well. Add the eggs, one at a time, and mix. Add the coconut with the remaining 1 cup flour and mix well. Add the vanilla and blend.

3. Pour the batter into the prepared pan. Bang the pan on the counter a couple of times to get rid of any air bubbles. Bake the cake for 1 hour and 15 minutes.

4. Remove the cake from the oven and set aside to cool for about 10 minutes. Meanwhile, make the glaze: In a small saucepan, simmer the sugar with ½ cup water until the sugar has dissolved, about 10 minutes. Stir in the coconut extract.

5. Run a knife around the outside edge of the cake. Remove the outer rim from the tube pan. While the cake is still hot, prick the top with the tines of a fork, and spoon the glaze over the top. Cool the cake on a wire rack.

6. Run the knife around the inner tube of the pan and under the bottom of the cake to loosen it. Take a plate and invert the cake onto it. Remove the bottom of the pan, then turn the cake back over so that the glazed part is on top. When completely cool, you can ice with 7-Minute Frosting. Store in an airtight container and serve at room temperature. Refrigerate leftovers.

Makes 12 to 16 servings

7-MINUTE FROSTING

2 egg whites
2 teaspoons light corn syrup
Dash of salt
1 teaspoon vanilla extract
⅓ cup toasted coconut, for
    garnish

Place the egg whites, corn syrup, salt, and ½ cup cold water into the top of a double boiler. With an electric mixer, whip the ingredients for 1 minute. Cook over gently boiling water, beating with the electric mixer, until the frosting forms stiff peaks, about 7 minutes. Remove the top of the double boiler and add the vanilla to the frosting. Continue beating the frosting for 2 minutes more, until the frosting reaches spreading consistency. Frost the top and sides of the cooled coconut cake, then sprinkle with the toasted coconut.

❖ BRANDON'S DECORATING TIPS ❖

Paula likes to use greenery and fresh fruit at Christmas. Use whatever looks fresh and pretty, either from your garden or the florist. Use the fresh fruit of the season—oranges and limes and other citrus, and apples, and nuts, all different kinds. I love big bowls of oranges that have been studded with whole cloves—they smell so good when people walk in. Hollow out artichokes and put a nice pillar candle in the center. Make bundles of asparagus tied together with raffia, with a tapered candle in the center, and place up and down the dining table. These are just beautiful!

Metric Equivalencies

LIQUID EQUIVALENCIES

CUSTOMARY	METRIC
¼ teaspoon	1.25 milliliters
½ teaspoon	2.5 milliliters
1 teaspoon	5 milliliters
1 tablespoon	15 milliliters
1 fluid ounce	30 milliliters
¼ cup	60 milliliters
⅓ cup	80 milliliters
½ cup	120 milliliters
1 cup	240 milliliters
1 pint (2 cups)	480 milliliters
1 quart (4 cups)	960 milliliters (.96 liter)
1 gallon (4 quarts)	3.84 liters

DRY MEASURE EQUIVALENCIES

CUSTOMARY	METRIC
1 ounce (by weight)	28 grams
¼ pound (4 ounces)	114 grams
1 pound (16 ounces)	454 grams
2.2 pounds	1 kilogram (1,000 grams)

OVEN TEMPERATURE EQUIVALENCIES

DESCRIPTION	° FAHRENHEIT	° CELSIUS
Cool	200	90
Very slow	250	120
Slow	300–325	150–160
Moderately slow	325–350	160–180
Moderate	350–375	180–190
Moderately hot	375–400	190–200
Hot	400–450	200–230
Very hot	450–500	230–260

Index

A

Ambrosia, 173
appetizers:
  Asparagus with Curry Dip, 88
  Black-eyed Pea Dip, 19
  Blue Cheese Dressing, 185
  Chicken Wings, Teriyaki and
    Buffalo, 184
  Collard Green Wontons, 6–7
  Corn Chowder, 181–82
  Crabbies, 145
  Crab-Stuffed Shrimp, The
    Lady & Sons, 34–35
  Cranberry Holiday Brie,
    205–6
  Guacamole, 110
  Macho Nachos, 109
  Olive Puffs, Baked, 135–36
  Phyllo Cups Filled with
    Chicken Salad, 86
  Phyllo Cups Filled with
    Shrimp Salad, 87
  Reubens, Mini, 68
  Salsa, Homemade, 110
  Shrimp and Lobster Bisque,
    36
  Shrimp Dip, Pink, 185
  Smoked Oyster Log, 136
  Taco Soup, 182
apple:
  Chicken Salad with Red
    Grapes, 101
  Cranberry, and Walnut Salad,
    101
  Fresh, Cake, 174

Rum Raisin–, Topping for Ice
  Cream, 22
Arroz con Tomate (Red Rice), 112
artichoke candle holders, 212
asparagus:
  candle holders, 212
  with Curry Dip, 88
  Phyllo-Wrapped, 39
Aunt Glynnis Hiers, 133
Aunt Jessie Ruth Sammons,
  115, 163
Aunt Peggy Paul Ort, 85, 115,
  123
Aunt Trina Beardon, 115
avocados, in Guacamole, 110

B

bacon:
  Brussels Sprouts with Onion
    and, 210
  and Scallops Pizza, 159
The Bag Lady, 86, 202
banana(s):
  Ambrosia, 173
  decorating with, in honor of
    Elvis, 31
  Hummingbird Cake, 13
  and Peanut Butter Sandwich,
    Fried, 31
  Pudding, Old-fashioned, 29
barbecue, *see* grill parties
Basil Cream Sauce, 35
beans (legumes):
  Black-eyed Pea Dip, 19

Black-eyed Peas (for Good
  Luck) with Hog Jowl (for
  Health), 18
  Hoppin' John, 15, 18
  Macho Nachos, 109
  Pinto Beans, Slow Cooker,
    147
  Red Beans and Rice, 55
  Succotash, 78
  Taco Soup, 182
Beans, Pole, Southern, 170
beef:
  Brisket, Texas, 146
  Cheeseburger Pies, Jamie's,
    186
  chicken-fried steak, 25
  Country-Fried Steak with
    Gravy, 25–26
  Goulash, Bobby's, 104
  Standing Rib Roast, 207
  Steak and Mushroom
    Topping (for potatoes), 127
  Taco Soup, 182
  Tenderloin, Soy-Rubbed, 208
  Tenderloin, Stuffed, 37
Beignets, French Quarter, 61–62
Bethesda Chapel, at Bethesda
  Home for Boys, Savannah,
  Ga., 63
beverages:
  Café au Lait, 62
  Irish Coffee, 14
  Margaritas, 107
  Mimosas, 14
  Russian Spiced Tea, 193

beverages (*cont.*)
    Sangria, 106
    Yogurt Smoothies, 102
Big Easy Mardi Gras, 49–62
biscuits:
    Buttermilk, 28
    Sausage, 89
    Sweet Potato, 56
Bisque, Shrimp and Lobster, 36
black-eyed pea(s):
    Dip, 19
    Hoppin' John, 15, 18
    (for Good Luck) with Hog
        Jowl (for Health), 18
Bloom, Orlando, 195
blueberry(ies):
    Flag Cake, 151
    Gems, 11
Blue Cheese Dressing, 185
Bobby's Goulash, 104
Boil, Low-Country, 149–50
Boursin, in Cream Cheese–
    Stuffed New Potatoes, 91
box lunches, 139
Branch, Brandon, 2, 14, 22, 31,
    42, 74, 83, 94, 114, 132,
    162, 178, 188, 201, 212
bread(s):
    Butterhorns, 81
    Corn, Dressing, Southern,
        167
    Parmesan Scones, 71
    Pudding, Krispy Kreme, with
        Rum Sauce, 60
    see also biscuits; muffins
Brie, Cranberry Holiday, 205–6
Brisket, Texas, 146
Brown Gravy, 166
Brownies, Crème de Menthe, 73
brunch:
    Asparagus with Curry Dip, 88
    Blueberry Gems, 11
    Collard Green Wontons, 6–7
    Crab and Spinach Casserole, 8
    Cream Cheese–Stuffed New
        Potatoes, 91
    Deviled Eggs, 90

    Hash Brown Casserole, 10
    Hummingbird Cake, 13
    Irish Coffee, 14
    Mimosas, 14
    New Year's Eve, 5–14
    Pecan Pie Muffins, 12
    Phyllo Cups Filled with
        Chicken Salad, 86
    Phyllo Cups Filled with
        Shrimp Salad, 87
    Sausage Biscuits, 89
    Sausage Casserole, Penny
        Smith's, 46
    Spinach-Swiss Casserole, 79
    Tomatoes, Baked, 9
    Yogurt Smoothies, 102
Brussels Sprouts with Onion
    and Bacon, 210
Buffalo and Teriyaki Chicken
    Wings, 184
butter:
    Cake, Toffee Gooey, 188
    Cakes, Peanut Butter Gooey,
        Elvis, 30
    Cinnamon-Honey, 200
    Herb, 201
    Orange-Ginger, 200
    Rum Sauce, 60
butter beans, in Succotash, 78
Butterhorns, 81
Buttermilk Biscuits, 28

C
cabbage:
    Country, 27
    Creamy, 47
    Hot Slaw, 148
Café au Lait, 62
cakes:
    Apple, Fresh, 174
    Carrot, 82
    Coconut Pound, with 7-
        Minute Frosting, 211–12
    Flag, 151
    Hummingbird, 13
    Icebox Fruitcake, 199

    Mardi Gras King, 57–59
    Molten Lava, 40
    Peanut Butter Gooey Butter,
        Elvis, 30
    Petits Fours, 94
    Pumpkin Cheesecake, 176
    Savannah Sheet, 130
    Toffee Gooey Butter, 188
    White, with Strawberry Icing,
        99
candy and confections:
    Georgia Cookie, 162
    Peppermint Bark, 195
    Pretzel-Peanut Bark, 196
caramel:
    Corn, Oven, 198
    Turtle Pizza, 161
carnation topiaries, 102
Carrot Cake, 82
Carter, Jimmy, 43–44, 48
casseroles:
    Crab and Spinach, 8
    Enchiladas de Pollo (Cream
        Cheese and Chicken
        Enchiladas), 111
    Hash Brown, 10
    Potato, Twice-Baked, 209
    Sausage, Penny Smith's, 46
    Spinach-Swiss, 79
    Turkey and Stuffing, 178
celebrations:
    Big Easy Mardi Gras, 49–62
    Christmas Dinner, 203–12
    Cinco de Mayo Fiesta,
        105–14
    Easter Dinner, 75–83
    Easter Egg Hunt, 85–94
    Elvis's Birthday, 23–31
    Father's Day Boating Picnic,
        133–39
    Fourth of July Outdoor Grill
        Party and Low-Country
        Boil, 143–52
    Graduation Potato Bar,
        123–32
    Homemade Christmas Gifts,
        189–201

May Day Pink and White
    Party, 95–102
Mother's Day Tea, 115–22
Movie-Watching Pizza Party
    in Bed, 153–62
My Wedding Anniversary, 63
New Year's Day Good Luck
    Meal, 15–22
New Year's Eve Brunch, 5–14
Presidents' Day, 43–48
St. Patrick's Day, 67–74
Sunday Afternoon Football
    Party, 179–88
Thanksgiving, 163–78
Valentine's Day, 33–42
champagne, in Mimosas, 14
Charles, Dora, 66
Cheddar cheese:
    Baked Olive Puffs, 135–36
    Cheese Sandwiches, 120
    Cheese Straws, 197
    Chili-Cheese Corn Muffins,
        183
    Crabbies, 145
    Creamy Macaroni and
        Cheese, 168
    Twice-Baked Potato
        Casserole, 209
cheese:
    Blue, Dressing, 185
    Brie, Cranberry Holiday,
        205–6
    Chili-, Corn Muffins, 183
    Feta and Pesto Pizza, 158
    Green Chili Squares, 108
    Macaroni and, Creamy, 168
    Macho Nachos, 109
    Sandwiches, 120
    Straws, 197
    see also Cheddar cheese; cream
        cheese
Cheeseburger Pies, Jamie's, 186
Cheesecake, Pumpkin, 176
cherry(ies):
    Cream Cheese and,
        Sandwiches, 97
    maraschino, in Ambrosia, 173

chicken:
    Apple Salad with Red Grapes,
        101
    Enchiladas de Pollo (Cream
        Cheese and Chicken
        Enchiladas), 111
    Grilled, Pita, 137–38
    Jambalaya, 53
    à la King Topping (for
        potatoes), 126
    Potpie, 177–78
    Salad, Phyllo Cups Filled
        with, 86
    Turducken, 165–66
    Wings, Teriyaki and Buffalo,
        184
chicken-fried steak, 25
chicory coffee, in Café au Lait,
    62
chili(es):
    -Cheese Corn Muffins, 183
    Green, Squares, 108
    Homemade Salsa, 110
    Macho Nachos, 109
    Sauce, 187
chocolate:
    Bundles with Chocolate
        Sauce, 41
    Chewy Cookies, 139
    Chip–Coffee Cookies, 131
    Crème de Menthe Brownies,
        73
    Double-, Cream Pie, 175
    Georgia Cookie Candy,
        162
    Icing, 73
    Miss Helen's Easter Eggs,
        92
    Molten Lava Cakes, 40
    Pecan Icing, 130
    Savannah Sheet Cake, 130
    Turtle Pizza, 161
    see also white chocolate
Chowder, Corn, 181–82
Christmas, 202
Christmas Dinner, 203–12
    decorating tips for, 212

Christmas gifts, homemade,
    189–201
    Cheese Straws, 197
    Cinnamon-Honey Butter, 200
    decorating tips for, 201
    Fruited Rice Curry Mix, 191
    Greek Salad Dressing, 194
    Herb Butter, 201
    Icebox Fruitcake, 199
    Lemon-Dill Rice Mix, 192
    Orange-Ginger Butter, 200
    Oven Caramel Corn, 198
    Peppermint Bark, 195
    Pretzel-Peanut Bark, 196
    Russian Spiced Tea, 193
Cinco de Mayo Fiesta, 105–14
    decorating tips for, 114
Cinnamon-Honey Butter, 200
Cocktail Sauce, 150
coconut:
    Ambrosia, 173
    Pound Cake with 7-Minute
        Frosting, 211–12
coffee:
    chicory, in Café au Lait, 62
    Chocolate Chip Cookies, 131
    ice cream, in Mud Pie, 152
    Irish, 14
collard green(s):
    for Good Cash Flow, 20
    and Ham Hock Pizza, 157
    Wontons, 6–7
Colored Sugar, 57–58
cookie(s):
    Candy, Georgia, 162
    Chocolate Chewy, 139
    Chocolate Chip–Coffee, 131
    Pecan Squares, 118
    Petticoat Tails, 117
Cooking with Paula Deen, 33,
    92
corn:
    Chowder, 181–82
    Low-Country Boil, 149–50
    Oven Caramel, 198
    Succotash, 78
    Taco Soup, 182

corn bread:
  Dressing, Southern, 167
  Muffins, 21
  Muffins, Chili-Cheese, 183
corned beef, in Mini Reubens,
  68
Country Cabbage, 27
Country-Fried Steak with
  Gravy, 25–26
crab(meat):
  Crabbies, 145
  Creamed Seafood Topping
    (for potatoes), 128
  Jambalaya, 53
  and Spinach Casserole, 8
  -Stuffed Shrimp, The Lady &
    Sons, 34–35
Crabbies, 145
cranberry:
  Apple, and Walnut Salad, 101
  Holiday Brie, 205–6
  Sauce, Stuffed, 172
cream cheese:
  and Cherry Sandwiches, 97
  Enchiladas de Pollo (Cream
    Cheese and Chicken
    Enchiladas), 111
  Ginger-Nut Sandwiches, 122
  Icing, 13, 82
  Smoked Oyster Log, 136
  –Stuffed New Potatoes, 91
  Twice-Baked Potato
    Casserole, 209
Creamed Seafood Topping (for
  potatoes), 128
Creamy Cabbage, 47
Creamy Macaroni and Cheese,
  168
Crème de Menthe Brownies,
  73
Crimes, Maggie, 44
Crowe, Cameron, 153, 155
Cruise, Tom, 153
Cucumber Sandwiches, 121
curry:
  Dip, Asparagus with, 88
  Mix, Fruited Rice, 191

D
Decorative Icing, 92
Deen, Bobby, 85, 103, 104,
  143, 144, 164, 179, 180,
  202
Deen, Brooke, 179–80, 202
Deen, Jamie, 143, 164, 179–80,
  189, 202
desserts:
  Ambrosia, 173
  Banana Pudding, Old-
    fashioned, 29
  Chocolate Bundles with
    Chocolate Sauce, 41
  Chocolate Chewy Cookies,
    139
  Chocolate Chip–Coffee
    Cookies, 131
  Crème de Menthe Brownies,
    73
  Double-Chocolate Cream Pie,
    175
  Easter Eggs, Miss Helen's,
    92–93
  French Quarter Beignets,
    61–62
  Georgia Cookie Candy,
    162
  Green Grits Pie, 72
  Krispy Kreme Bread Pudding
    with Rum Sauce, 60
  Lemon Cups, 119
  Margarita Mousse, 113
  Mud Pie, 152
  Peach Ice Cream, Easy, 48
  Peanut Butter Ice Cream,
    48
  Pecan Squares, 118
  Petits Fours, 94
  Petticoat Tails, 117
  Pretzels Dipped in White
    Chocolate, 98
  Pumpkin Cheesecake, 176
  Rum Raisin–Apple Topping
    for Ice Cream, 22
  Strawberries Dipped in White
    Chocolate, 98

  Strawberry Pizza, 160
  Turtle Pizza, 161
  see also cakes
Deviled Eggs, 90
Deviled Oysters, 169
Dill-Lemon Rice Mix, 192
dips:
  Black-eyed Pea, 19
  Blue Cheese Dressing, 185
  Curry, 88
  Guacamole, 110
  Salsa, Homemade, 110
  Shrimp, Pink, 185
Dora's Oxtails, 66
Double-Chocolate Cream Pie,
  175
Downtown Garden Club of
  Savannah, Ga., 116
Dressing, Corn Bread,
  Southern, 167
dressings (salad):
  Blue Cheese, 185
  Greek Salad, 194
drinks, *see* beverages
driveway, lining with votive
  lights, 178
dry measure equivalencies, 213
duck, in Turducken, 165–66
Dunst, Kirsten, 195

E
Easter baskets, 85, 94
Easter Dinner, 75–83
  decorating tips for, 83
Easter Egg Hunt, 85–94
  decorating tips for, 94
Easter Eggs, Miss Helen's,
  92–93
eggs:
  Deviled, 90
  Easter, Miss Helen's, 92–93
  Hash Brown Casserole, 10
  raw or lightly cooked,
    warning against, 114
Elizabethtown, 153–54, 155,
  195

Elvis Peanut Butter Gooey Butter Cakes, 30
Elvis's Birthday, 23–31
  decorating tips for, 31
Enchiladas de Pollo (Cream Cheese and Chicken Enchiladas), 111

F
Father's Day Boating Picnic, 133–39
  decorating tips for, 139
Feta and Pesto Pizza, 158
Flag Cake, 151
flowers, decorating tips for, 14, 42, 83, 102, 132, 162
Food Network, 44, 164, 186
  kitchen makeover contest of, 154
Football Party, Sunday Afternoon, 179–88
Fourth of July:
  decorating tips for, 152
  Flag Cake for, 151
  Outdoor Grill Party and Low-Country Boil, 143–52
French Quarter Beignets, 61–62
Fried Onion Rings with Chili Sauce, 187
Fried Peanut Butter and Banana Sandwich, 31
frostings:
  7-Minute, 212
  see also icings
fruit, decorating with, 14, 31, 212
Fruitcake, Icebox, 199
Fruited Rice Curry Mix, 191

G
Garlic Mashed Potatoes, 38
Georgia Cookie Candy, 162
gifts:
  decorating tips for, 201
  see also Christmas gifts, homemade

ginger:
  -Nut Sandwiches, 122
  Orange-, Butter, 200
Goulash, Bobby's, 104
Graduation Potato Bar, 123–32
  decorating tips for, 132
Grapes, Red, Apple Chicken Salad with, 101
Gravy, Brown, 166
Greek Salad Dressing, 194
Green Chili Squares, 108
Green Grits Pie, 72
Greenlee, Lori, 49
Green Peas, 70
Greer, Judy, 195
Grilled Brisket, Texas, 146
Grilled Chicken Pita, 137–38
grill parties:
  Crabbies, 145
  Fourth of July Outdoor Grill Party and Low-Country Boil, 143–52
  Hot Slaw, 148
  Pinto Beans, Slow Cooker, 147
  Texas Brisket, 146
grits:
  Green, Pie, 72
  Whipping-Cream, 47
Groover, Anthony, 65, 85
Groover, Father Hank, 49–50
Groover, Michael, 1–2, 33, 37, 41, 49, 63, 65, 113, 133–34, 140, 143, 149, 155, 164, 179
Groover, Michelle, 65, 85
Guacamole, 110

H
ham:
  Hock and Collard Green Pizza, 157
  Muffuletta Sandwiches, 51–52
  Peanut Butter–Glazed, 77

Salad, 83
Salad Sandwiches, 121
Hash Brown(s), 91
  Casserole, 10
herb:
  Butter, 201
  -Crusted Pork Loin, 17
Hiers, Beth, 163
Hiers, Bob, 163
Hiers, Corrie, 115–16, 203
Hiers, Dawn, 203
Hiers, Earl "Bubba," 75, 140–41, 179, 203
Hiers, Earl Wayne, Sr., 133
Hiers, Grandmother, 115
Hiers, Jill, 115–16
high school graduation, celebration for, 123–32
Hog Jowl (for Health), Black-eyed Peas (for Good Luck) with, 18
Honey-Cinnamon Butter, 200
Hoppin' John, 15, 18
Hot Slaw, 148
House Seasoning, 147
Hummingbird Cake, 13
Hurricane Katrina, 49–50

I
Icebox Fruitcake, 199
ice cream:
  coffee, in Mud Pie, 152
  Peach, Easy, 48
  Peanut Butter, 48
  Rum Raisin–Apple Topping for, 22
icings:
  Chocolate, 73
  Chocolate-Pecan, 130
  Cream Cheese, 13, 82
  Decorative, 92
  Strawberry, 99
  White, 57–58
Irish Coffee, 14

J
Jambalaya, 53
Jamie's Cheeseburger Pies, 186

K
Krispy Kreme Bread Pudding
    with Rum Sauce, 60

L
Lady & Sons Restaurant,
    Savannah, Ga., 66, 140
Lamas, Billy and Kathy, 5
Lamb Stew, 69
lemon(s):
    Cups, 119
    -Dill Rice Mix, 192
    Mardi Gras King Cake, 57–59
    votive candle holders, 14
Leven, Gail, 153
lima beans, in Succotash, 78
lime(s):
    Margarita Mousse, 113
    votive candle holders, 14,
      74
liquid equivalencies, 213
Lobster and Shrimp Bisque, 36
Low-Country Boil, 149–50
lunches:
    packing as box lunches for
      men, 139
    see also picnics

M
macaroni:
    Bobby's Goulash, 104
    and Cheese, Creamy, 168
    Salad, 138
Macho Nachos, 109
Magnolia Hunting and Fishing
    Lodge, Crystal River, Fla.,
    23
main dishes:
    Beef Tenderloin, Stuffed, 37
    Brisket, Texas, 146

Cheeseburger Pies, Jamie's,
    186
Chicken Potpie, 177–78
Enchiladas de Pollo (Cream
    Cheese and Chicken
    Enchiladas), 111
Ham, Peanut Butter–Glazed,
    77
Jambalaya, 53
Lamb Stew, 69
Oxtails, Dora's, 66
Pork Loin, Herb-Crusted, 17
Potatoes, Baked, with
    Traditional Toppings,
    125–28
Quail, Oyster-Stuffed, 45
Shrimp Étouffée, 54
Standing Rib Roast, 207
Steak, Country-Fried, with
    Gravy, 25–26
Tenderloin, Soy-Rubbed,
    208
Turducken, 165–66
Turkey and Stuffing
    Casserole, 178
Marcus, Michael, 40
Mardi Gras, Big Easy, 49–62
Mardi Gras King Cake, 57–59
Margarita(s), 107
    Mousse, 113
May Day Pink and White Party,
    95–102
    decorating tips for, 102
metric equivalencies, 213
Mexican:
    Arroz con Tomate (Red Rice),
      112
    Cinco de Mayo Fiesta,
      105–14
    Enchiladas de Pollo (Cream
      Cheese and Chicken
      Enchiladas), 111
    Green Chili Squares, 108
    Guacamole, 110
    Macho Nachos, 109
    Margarita Mousse, 113
    Margaritas, 107

Salsa, Homemade, 110
Sangria, 106
Mimosas, 14
Mini Reubens, 68
Miss Helen's Easter Eggs, 92–93
Molten Lava Cakes, 40
Mom's Kitchen, Plains, Ga., 44
Mother's Day Tea, 115–22
Mousse, Margarita, 113
Movie-Watching Pizza Party in
    Bed, 153–62
    decorating tips for, 162
Mud Pie, 152
muffins:
    Blueberry Gems, 11
    Corn, Chili-Cheese, 183
    Corn Bread, 21
    Pecan Pie, 12
Muffuletta Sandwiches, 51–52
Mushroom and Steak Topping
    (for potatoes), 127
Mystic Pizza, 154
Mystic Pizza, Mystic, Conn.,
    154–55, 157
My Wedding Anniversary, 63

N
Nesbit, Martha, 2
New Orleans:
    Big Easy Mardi Gras, 49–62
    Café au Lait, 62
    French Quarter Beignets,
      61–62
    Hurricane Katrina and,
      49–50
    Jambalaya, 53
    Krispy Kreme Bread Pudding
      with Rum Sauce, 60
    Mardi Gras King Cake, 57–59
    Muffuletta Sandwiches,
      51–52
    Red Beans and Rice, 55
    Shrimp Étouffée, 54
New Year's Day Good Luck
    Meal, 15–22
    decorating tips for, 22

New Year's Eve Brunch, 5–14
decorating tips for, 14
New Year's resolutions, 16
Nicholson, Bill, 60
nut(s):
decorating with, 212
Ginger-, Sandwiches, 122
see also pecan(s)

O
Old-fashioned Banana Pudding, 29
olive:
Puffs, Baked, 135–36
Salad, 51
onion(s):
Brussels Sprouts with Bacon and, 210
Rings, Fried, with Chili Sauce, 187
orange(s):
Ambrosia, 173
decorations, for Christmas, 212
-Ginger Butter, 200
juice, in Mimosas, 14
Oven Caramel Corn, 198
oven temperature equivalencies, 213
Oxtails, Dora's, 66
oyster(s):
Deviled, 169
Jambalaya, 53
Smoked, Log, 136
-Stuffed Quail, 45

P
Paramount Studios, 153–54
Parmesan Scones, 71
pasta, *see* macaroni
Paul, Granddaddy, 5, 15, 23, 133
Paul, Grandmother, 23, 113, 115
Peach Ice Cream, Easy, 48

peanut butter:
and Banana Sandwich, Fried, 31
Georgia Cookie Candy, 162
–Glazed Ham, 77
Gooey Butter Cakes, Elvis, 30
Ice Cream, 48
Peanut-Pretzel Bark, 196
peas:
black-eyed, *see* black-eyed pea(s)
Green, 70
pecan(s):
Ambrosia, 173
Cheese Sandwiches, 120
Chocolate Icing, 130
Ginger-Nut Sandwiches, 122
Pie Muffins, 12
Smoked Oyster Log, 136
Squares, 118
Turtle Pizza, 161
Penny Smith's Sausage Casserole, 46
Peppermint Bark, 195
Pesto and Feta Pizza, 158
Petits Fours, 94
Petticoat Tails, 117
phyllo cups, 119
Filled with Chicken Salad, 86
Filled with Shrimp Salad, 87
Lemon Cups, 119
Phyllo-Wrapped Asparagus, 39
picnics:
Chocolate Chewy Cookies, 139
Deviled Eggs, 90
Father's Day Boating, 133–39
Grilled Chicken Pita, 137–38
Macaroni Salad, 138
Mini Reubens, 68
Olive Puffs, Baked, 135–36
Smoked Oyster Log, 136
pies (dessert):
Double-Chocolate Cream, 175
Green Grits, 72
Mud, 152

pies (savory):
Cheeseburger, Jamie's, 186
Chicken Potpie, 177–78
pineapple:
Ambrosia, 173
Hummingbird Cake, 13
Pink Shrimp Dip, 185
Pinto Beans, Slow Cooker, 147
Pita, Grilled Chicken, 137–38
pizza:
Collard Green and Ham Hock, 157
Dough, Basic, 156–57
Movie-Watching Pizza Party in Bed, 153–62
Pesto and Feta, 158
Scallops and Bacon, 159
Strawberry, 160
Turtle, 161
Plain Peanuts, Plains, Ga., 44, 48
Plains, Ga., Better Hometown Program, 44
Pole Beans, Southern, 170
popcorn:
decorating tub for, 162
Oven Caramel, 198
Pork Loin, Herb-Crusted, 17
potato(es):
Baked, with Traditional Toppings, 125–28
Chicken à la King Topping for, 126
Creamed Seafood Topping for, 128
Garlic Mashed, 38
Hash Brown Casserole, 10
Hash Browns, 91
Low-Country Boil, 149–50
Miss Helen's Easter Eggs, 92–93
New, Cream Cheese–Stuffed, 91
Sauce, 150
Steak and Mushroom Topping for, 127
Twice-Baked, Casserole, 209

Potpie, Chicken, 177–78
Pound Cake, Coconut, with 7-Minute Frosting, 211–12
Presidents' Day, 43–48
Presley, Elvis, 23, 24, 31
    birthday celebration for, 23–31
pretzel(s):
    Dipped in White Chocolate, 98
    Peanut Bark, 196
Proffitt, Brian, 30
provolone cheese, in Muffuletta Sandwiches, 51–52
puddings:
    Banana, Old-fashioned, 29
    Krispy Kreme Bread, with Rum Sauce, 60
puff pastry:
    Chocolate Bundles with Chocolate Sauce, 41
    Cranberry Holiday Brie, 205–6
    Jamie's Cheeseburger Pies, 186
Puffs, Olive, Baked, 135–36
Pumpkin Cheesecake, 176
pumpkin seeds, in Oven Caramel Corn, 198

Q
Quail, Oyster-Stuffed, 45

R
raisins, in Rum Raisin–Apple Topping for Ice Cream, 22
Red Beans and Rice, 55
Red Rice (Arroz con Tomate), 112
Reubens, Mini, 68
Rib Roast, Standing, 207
rice:
    Arroz con Tomate (Red Rice), 112
    Hoppin' John, 15, 18

Jambalaya, 53
    Mix, Fruited Curry, 191
    Mix, Lemon-Dill, 192
    Red Beans and, 55
    White, 26
Roberts, Julia, 154
roses, keeping fresh, 42
roux, 54
rum:
    Butter, Sauce, 60
    Raisin–Apple Topping for Ice Cream, 22
Russian Spiced Tea, 193

S
St. Patrick's Day, 67–74
    decorating tips for, 74
Salad Dressing, Greek, 194
salads:
    Apple, Cranberry, and Walnut, 101
    Apple Chicken, with Red Grapes, 101
    Chicken, Phyllo Cups Filled with, 86
    Ham, 83
    Macaroni, 138
    Olive, 51
    Shrimp, Phyllo Cups Filled with, 87
    Spinach, 129
    Spinach and Strawberry, 100
salami, in Muffuletta Sandwiches, 51–52
Salsa, Homemade, 110
Salter, Bobby, 44, 48
sandwich(es):
    Cream Cheese and Cherry, 97
    Fried Peanut Butter and Banana, 31
    Grilled Chicken Pita, 137–38
    Mini Reubens, 68
    Muffuletta, 51–52
sandwiches, tea:
    Cheese, 120
    Cucumber, 121

Ginger-Nut, 122
    Ham Salad, 121
Sangria, 106
sauces:
    Basil Cream, 35
    Brown Gravy, 166
    Buffalo, 184
    Butter-Rum, 60
    Chili, 187
    Chocolate, 41
    Cocktail, 150
    Cranberry, Stuffed, 172
    Potato, 150
    Tartar, 150
    Teriyaki, 184
    Yogurt, 137
sauerkraut, in Mini Reubens, 68
sausage:
    Biscuits, 89
    Casserole, Penny Smith's, 46
    Hash Brown Casserole, 10
    Jambalaya, 53
    Low-Country Boil, 149–50
    Savannah Sheet Cake, 130
    Scallops and Bacon Pizza, 159
    Scones, Parmesan, 71
seafood:
    Creamed, Topping (for potatoes), 128
    Jambalaya, 53
    Oysters, Deviled, 169
    Scallops and Bacon Pizza, 159
    see also crab(meat); shrimp
Seasoning, House, 147
7-Minute Frosting, 212
Sheet Cake, Savannah, 130
shortbread cookies (Petticoat Tails), 117
shrimp:
    Crab-Stuffed, The Lady & Sons, 34–35
    Creamed Seafood Topping (for potatoes), 128
    Dip, Pink, 185
    Étouffée, 54
    Jambalaya, 53

and Lobster Bisque, 36
Low-Country Boil, 149–50
Salad, Phyllo Cups Filled
    with, 87
side dishes:
    Apple, Cranberry, and
        Walnut Salad, 101
    Arroz con Tomate (Red Rice),
        112
    Black-eyed Peas (for Good
        Luck) with Hog Jowl (for
        Health), 18
    Brussels Sprouts with Onion
        and Bacon, 210
    Butterhorns, 81
    Buttermilk Biscuits, 28
    Cabbage, Country, 27
    Cabbage, Creamy, 47
    Chili-Cheese Corn Muffins,
        183
    Collard or Turnip Greens (for
        Good Cash Flow), 20
    Corn Bread Dressing,
        Southern, 167
    Fruited Rice Curry Mix, 191
    Green Chili Squares, 108
    Green Peas, 70
    Grits, Whipping-Cream, 47
    Lemon-Dill Rice Mix, 192
    Macaroni and Cheese,
        Creamy, 168
    Macaroni Salad, 138
    Onion Rings, Fried, with
        Chili Sauce, 187
    Oysters, Deviled, 169
    Phyllo-Wrapped Asparagus,
        39
    Pinto Beans, Slow Cooker,
        147
    Pole Beans, Southern, 170
    Potatoes, Garlic Mashed, 38
    Red Beans and Rice, 55
    Sausage Casserole, Penny
        Smith's, 46
    Slaw, Hot, 148
    Spinach and Strawberry
        Salad, 100

Spinach Salad, 129
Squash Boats, 80
Succotash, 78
Sweet Potato Biscuits, 56
Sweet Potatoes, Baked, with
    Butter and Brown Sugar,
    171
Tomatoes, Baked, 9
Twice-Baked Potato
    Casserole, 209
White Rice, 26
Slaw, Hot, 148
Slow Cooker Pinto Beans, 147
Smith, Penny, 46, 48
Smoked Oyster Log, 136
Smoothies, Yogurt, 102
soups:
    Corn Chowder, 181–82
    Shrimp and Lobster Bisque,
        36
    Taco, 182
Soy-Rubbed Tenderloin, 208
Spiced Tea, Russian, 193
spinach:
    and Crab Casserole, 8
    Salad, 129
    and Strawberry Salad, 100
    -Swiss Casserole, 79
spreads:
    Cinnamon-Honey Butter, 200
    Herb Butter, 201
    Orange-Ginger Butter, 200
    Smoked Oyster Log, 136
Squash Boats, 80
Standing Rib Roast, 207
steak:
    chicken-fried, 25
    Country-Fried, with Gravy,
        25–26
    and Mushroom Topping (for
        potatoes), 127
Stew, Lamb, 69
strawberry(ies):
    Dipped in White Chocolate,
        98
    Flag Cake, 151
    Icing, White Cake with, 99

Pizza, 160
    and Spinach Salad, 100
    Yogurt Smoothies, 102
Stuffed Beef Tenderloin, 37
Stuffed Cranberry Sauce, 172
Stuffing, Turkey and, Casserole,
    178
Succotash, 78
Sugar, Colored, 57–58
Sunday Afternoon Football
    Party, 179–88
    decorating tips for, 188
sunflower seeds, in Oven
    Caramel Corn, 198
sweet potato(es):
    Baked, with Butter and
        Brown Sugar, 171
    Biscuits, 56
Swiss cheese:
    Mini Reubens, 68
    Spinach Casserole, 79

T
Taco Soup, 182
Tartar Sauce, 150
tea, afternoon:
    Cheese Sandwiches, 120
    Cucumber Sandwiches,
        121
    Ginger-Nut Sandwiches,
        122
    Ham Sandwiches, 121
    Lemon Cups, 119
    Mother's Day, 115–22
    Pecan Squares, 118
    Petticoat Tails, 117
Tea, Russian Spiced, 193
tequila, in Margaritas, 107
Teriyaki and Buffalo Chicken
    Wings, 184
Texas Brisket, 146
Thanksgiving, 163–78
    decorating tips for, 178
toffee:
    Butter Cakes, Gooey, 188
    Mud Pie, 152

tomatoes:
  Arroz con Tomate (Red Rice), 112
  Baked, 9
  Homemade Salsa, 110
topiaries, carnation, 102
tortilla(s):
  chips, in Macho Nachos, 109
  Enchiladas de Pollo (Cream Cheese and Chicken Enchiladas), 111
  Turtle Pizza, 161
Toy House, Albany, Ga., 85
Turducken, 165–66
turkey:
  and Stuffing Casserole, 178
  Turducken, 165–66
Turnip Greens (for Good Cash Flow), 20
Turtle Pizza, 161
Twice-Baked Potato Casserole, 209

U
UGA, 179
Uncle Burney Hiers, 163
Uncle George Ort, 85, 123
University of Georgia football, 179–80

V
Valentine's Day, 33–42
  decorating for, 42
Vineyard, Jack, Charlotte, and Melanie, 44
votive candles, 14, 42, 74

W
Walnut, Apple, and Cranberry Salad, 101
Wedding Anniversary, 63
Whipping-Cream Grits, 47
whiskey, in Irish Coffee, 14
White Cake with Strawberry Icing, 99

white chocolate:
  Peppermint Bark, 195
  Pretzel-Peanut Bark, 196
  Pretzels Dipped in, 98
  Strawberries Dipped in, 98
White Icing, 57–58
White Rice, 26
wine, in Sangria, 106
Winfrey, Oprah, 43
Wontons, Collard Green, 6–7

Y
yellow squash, in Squash Boats, 80
yogurt:
  Sauce, 137
  Smoothies, 102

Z
zucchini, in Squash Boats, 80